STROUD'S JUDICIAL DICTIONARY OF
WORDS AND PHRASES

STROUD'S JUDICIAL DICTIONARY OF WORDS AND PHRASES

First Cumulative Supplement

Sixth Edition

AUSTRALIA
Law Book Co.
Sydney

CANADA AND USA
Carswell
Toronto

HONG KONG
Sweet & Maxwell Asia

NEW ZEALAND
Brookers
Wellington

SINGAPORE AND MALAYSIA
Sweet & Maxwell Asia
Singapore and Kuala Lumper

STROUD'S JUDICIAL DICTIONARY OF WORDS AND PHRASES

First Cumulative Supplement to the Sixth Edition Up-to-date to September 30, 2001

by DANIEL GREENBERG
of Lincoln's Inn, Barrister,
and of the Office of the Parliamentary Counsel

LONDON
SWEET & MAXWELL
2001

Published in 2002 by
Sweet & Maxwell Ltd of
100 Avenue Road, London NW3 3PF.
http://www.sweetandmaxwell.co.uk
Typeset by Mendip Communications Ltd, Frome, Somerset
Printed and bound in Great Britain by Antony Rowe Limited, Reading

No natural forests were destroyed to make this product; only farmed timber was
used and re-planted.

ISBN 0 421 76970 8

PREFACE

Here is the first of what is intended, as for the Fifth Edition, to be a series of cumulative annual supplements. This supplement mostly consists of cases reported and statutes published between the preparation of the Sixth Edition and the close of September 2001.

Due to a misunderstanding, the opening pages of the Sixth Edition did not contain an acknowledgement of the valuable services provided in the preparation of the new edition by Michael Hayes and Tim Styles. I take this opportunity of recording my gratitude to them for their conscientious labours without which the edition could not have been produced in the time allotted.

My approach in deciding what to include and exclude remains as stated in the preface to the Sixth Edition. I am continuing to include, sparingly, material from European cases and legislation, from academic writings and from appropriate Parliamentary and other papers.

The supplements to the sixth edition will differ from supplements to earlier editions in two ways.

First, I hope to use supplements as a way of continuing the work begun in the preparation of the sixth edition of clarifying and simplifying entries which have become lengthy and complicated over the years. Where an entry in a supplement should be treated as replacing rather than supplementing an entry in the main work this will be indicated in italics at the end of the entry.

Secondly, each supplement will include a short essay drawing attention to entries which are new to that supplement and which are of particular significance (whether by themselves or as evidence of a trend).

I will be very grateful for comments and suggestions on this supplement or the main work. They can be sent to my publishers, to whom I remain grateful for their kind and attentive treatment.

Daniel Greenberg
October 2001

Table of Abbreviations

Note. The use of SMALL CAPITALS throughout the book, suggests a reference to the word or phrase so printed.

Where dates are given in the last column of this table, that indicates that the item against which it appears is a series, or volume, of Reports of Cases, and these dates also indicate the period covered by such reports.

A

A.B.C.	Australian Bankruptcy Cases	*1928–1964*
A.C. (preceded by date)	Law Reports, Appeal Cases	*1891–*
A.L.J.	Australian Law Journal	*1927–*
A.L.R.	Argus Law Reports	*1895–1981*
A.L.R.	Australian Law Reports	*1982–*
A.L.J.R.	Australian Law Journal Reports	*1927–*
A.R. (N.S.W.)	Industrial Arbitration Reports, New South Wales	*1902–*
A. & E.	Adolphus and Ellis	*1834–1841*
Abbott	Abbott on Merchant Ships and Seamen	
Abb.	Abbott's United States Circuit Court Reports	
Addams	Addams Ecclesiastical Reports	*1822–1826*
Add. C	Addison on Contracts	
Add. T.	Addison on Torts	
Al. & N.	Alcock and Napier	
Ala.	Alabama Reports	
Aleyn	Aleyn	*1646–1649*
All E.R. (preceded by date)	All England Reports	*1936–*
Allen	Allen's Massachusetts Reports	
Amb	Ambler	*1737–1783*
And.	Anderson	*1558–1603*
Ann. Pr.	Annual Practice	
Anstr.	Anstruther	*1792–1796*
App. Cas.	Law Reports, Appeal Cases (*Note.* In and since 1891 these reports are cited by the year, e.g. [1891] A.C.)	*1875–1890*
Arch. Bank	Archbold on Bankruptcy	
Arch. Cr	Archbold's Pleading and Evidence in Criminal Cases	
Arch. P.L.	Archbold's Poor Law	
Arn.	Arnould on Marine Insurance	

Arnold	Arnold	*1838–1839*
art.	Article	
Asp.	Aspinall	*1871–1943*
Atk.	Atkyns	*1736–1755*
Att.-Gen., A.-G.	Attorney-General	

B

B.W.C.C.	Butterworth's Workmen's Compensation Cases	*1907–1949*
B. & Ad.	Barnewall and Adolphus	*1830–1834*
B. & Ald.	Barnewall and Alderson	*1817–1822*
B. & Aust.	Barron and Austin	*1842*
B. & C.	Barnewall and Cresswell	*1822–1830*
B. & F.	Broderick and Fremantle	*1840–1865*
B. & Macn.	Browne and Macnamara; but generally herein cited as Ry. & Can. Traffic Cas.	
B. & P.	Bosanquet and Puller	*1796–1804*
B. & P.N.R.	Bosanquet and Puller, New Reports	*1804–1807*
B. & S.	Best and Smith	*1861–1870*
Bac. Ab.	Bacon's Abridgment	
Bail C.C.	Bail Court Cases (sometimes called Lowndes & Maxwell)	*1852–1854*
Baldwin	Baldwin on Bankruptcy	
Ball & Beatty	Ball and Beatty	*1807–1814*
Barb. (N.Y.)	Barbour's New York Supreme Court Reports	
Barnardiston C.C.	Barnardiston's Chancery Cases	*1740–1741*
Barnes	Barnes' Notes of Cases	*1732–1760*
Baxter	Baxter's Tennessee Reports	
Bea.	Beavan	*1838–1866*
Beatty	Beatty	*1814–1836*
Bell C.C.	Bell, Crown Cases	*1858–1860*
Benedict	Benedict's United States District Court Reports	
Benj.	Benjamin on Sales of Personal Property	
Beven	Beven on Negligence in Law	
Bing.	Bingham	*1822–1834*
Bing. N.C.	Bingham, New Cases	*1834–1840*

Bl. Com.	Blackstone's Commentaries, the paging being that of the 5th ed.; the edition chiefly used being the 12th by Christian, wherein Blackstone's last paging is preserved in the margin	
Bl. H.	Blackstone, Henry	*1788–1796*
Bl. W.	Blackstone, William	*1746–1780*
Blackb.	Blackburn on Sales	
Bligh	Bligh's Reports of Cases in the House of Lords	*1819–1821*
Bligh N.S.	Bligh, New Series	*1827–1837*
Bott	Bott	*1768–1827*
Bowstead	Bowstead on Agency	
Bro. C.C.	Brown's Chancery Cases	*1778–1794*
Brod. & B.	Broderip & Bingham	*1819–1822*
Brown P.C.	Brown's Parliamentary Cases	*1702–1800*
Brown. & Lush.	Browning & Lushington	*1863–1866*
Brownl. & Gold.	Brownlow and Goldesborough	*1558–1625*
Buckl.	Buckley on the Companies Acts	
Build L.R.	Building Law Reports	*1976–*
Bulst.	Bulstrode	*1603–1649*
Bunb.	Bunbury	*1713–1742*
Burr.	Burrow	*1756–1772*
Burr S.C.	Burrow's Settlement Cases	*1732–1776*
Byles	Byles on Bills of Exchange and Promissory Notes	

C

c.	Chapter (of Act of Parliament)	
C.A.	Court of Appeal	
C.A.R.	Commonwealth Arbitration Reports	*1905–*
C.B.	Common Bench Reports	*1845–1856*
C.B.N.S.	Common Bench Reports — New Series	*1856–1865*
C.C.A.	Court of Criminal Appeal	
C.C.C.	Canadian Criminal Cases	*1893–*
C.C.R.	County Court Rules	
C.L.	Current Law Yearbooks	*1947–*
C.L.R.	Commonwealth Law Reports	*1903–*
C.L.Y.	Current Law Yearbook	
C.M.L.R.	Common Market Law Reports	*1962–*
C.P.D.	Law Reports, Common Pleas Division	*1875–1880*
C.P.R.	Canadian Patent Reports	*1939–*

C.R.	Criminal Reports (Canada)	*1946–1967*
C.R.N.S.	Criminal Reports (Canada) New Series	*1967–*
C.T.C.	Canada Tax Cases	
C. & K.	Carrington and Kirwan	*1843–1853*
C. & M.	Carrington and Marshman	*1841–1842*
C. & P.	Carrington and Payne	*1823–1841*
Ca. t. Hard.	Cases, temp. Hardwicke	*1733–1737*
Ca. t. Talb.	Cases in Equity, temp. Talbot	*1733–1737*
Cab. & El.	Cababe and Ellis	*1882–1885*
Cal.	California Reports	
Cald.	Caldecott's Settlement Cases	*1776–1785*
Callis	The Reading of Robert Callis on the Statute of Sewers, 23 Hen. 8, c. 5, delivered by him at Gray's Inn, August, 1622	
Camp.	Campbell	*1807–1816*
Carp.	Carpmael's Patent Cases	*1602–1842*
Carter	Carter	*1664–1676*
Carth.	Carthew	*1668–1701*
Carver	Carver on Carriage of Goods by Sea	
Ch. (preceded by date)	Law Reports, Chancery	*1891–*
Ch.	Law Reports, Chancery Appeals	*1865–1875*
Ch. Ca.	Cases in Chancery	*1660–1693*
Ch. D.	Law Reports, Chancery Division (*Note.* In and since 1891 these Reports are cited by the year and volume, e.g. [1891] 1 Ch.)	*1875–1890*
Ch. Rep.	Reports in Chancery	*1625–1710*
Challis	Challis on Real Property	
Chalmers	Chalmers on Bills of Exchange	
Chaney (Mich.)	Chaney's Michigan Reports	
Chitty	Chitty *Vol. I, 1819, Vol. II, 1770–1822*	
Chitty Eq. Ind.	Chitty's Equity Index	
Cl. & F.	Clarke and Finelly	*1831–1846*
Co. Litt.	Coke upon Littleton, the edition here used being the 18th by Hargrave & Butler	
Col.	Colorado Reports	
Coll.	Collyer	*1844–1846*
Colt, Reg. Cas.	Cotlman, Registration Cases	*1879–1885*
Com.	Comyn	*1696–1740*
Com. Cas.	Commercial Cases	*1895–*

Com. Dig.	Comyn's Digest	
Com. L.R.	Common Law Reports	*1854–1855*
Com. L.R. (preceded by date)	Commercial Law Reports	*1981–*
Con. & L.	Connor & Lawson	*1841–1843*
Conv. (N.S.)	Conveyancer and Property Lawyer (New 1936, current Series)	
Cooper, C.P.	Cooper, Charles Purton	*1837–1838*
Cooper, G.	Cooper, George	*1815, with a few earlier cases in and from 1792*
Cooper t. Broughham	Cooper, Charles Purton, temp. Brougham	*1833–1834*
Cooper t. Cott.	Cooper, Charles Purton, temp. Cottenham	*1846–1848*
Coote	Coote on Mortgages	
Cowel	Cowel's Interpreter by Tho. Tanley, 1672	
Cowen	Cowen's New York Reports	
Cowp.	Cowper	*1774–1778*
Cox C.C.	Cox's Criminal Cases	*1843–1945*
Cox Ch.	Cox's Chancery Cases	*1745–1797*
Cp.	Compare	
Cr.App.R.	Criminal Appeal Reports	*1908–*
Cr.L.Q.	Criminal Law Quarterly (Canada)	
Cr. M. & R.	Crompton, Meeson & Roscoe	*1834–1835*
Cr. & Dix	Crawford and Dix	*1839–1846*
Cr. & Dix Ab. Cas.	Crawford and Dix, Abridged Notes of Cases	*1837–1838*
Cr. & J.	Crompton and Jervis	*1830–1832*
Cr. & M.	Crompton and Meeson	*1832–1834*
Cr. & Ph.	Craig and Philip	*1840–1841*
Cranch	Cranch's United States Supreme Court Reports	
Crim. L.R.	Criminal Law Review	*1954–*
Cro. Car.	Croke, temp. Charles I	*1581–1641*
Cro. Eliz.	Croke, temp. Elizabeth	*1581–1641*
Cro. Jac.	Croke, temp. James I	*1581–1641*
Cru. Dig.	Cruise's Digest of the laws of England Respecting Real Property	
Cty. Ct.	County Court	
Cunningham	Cunningham's K.B. Cases, 3rd. ed.	*1734–1735*

Curt.	Curtels	*1834–1844*
Cush.	Cushing's Massachusetts Reports	

D

D.C.	Divisional Court	
D.G.	De Gex	*1844–1848*
D.G. & J.	De Gex and Jones	*1856–1859*
D.G. & S.	De Gex and Smale	*1846–1852*
D.G.F. & J.	De Gex, Fisher and Jones	*1859–1862*
D.J. & S.	De Gex, Jones and Smith	*1862–1865*
D.G.M. & G.	De Gex, Macnaughten and Gordon	*1851–1857*
D.L.R.	Dominion Law Reports	*1912–*
D.T.C.	Dominion Tax Cases	
D. & M.	Davison and Merivale	*1843–1844*
D. & R.	Dowling & Ryland	*1822–1827*
D. & Sw.	Deane and Swabey	*1855–1857*
Daly	Daly's New York Common Pleas Reports	
Dan. Ch. Pr.	Daniell's Chancery Practice	
Dart	Dart on Vendors and Purchasers	
Dea. & C.	Deacon & Chitty	*1832–1835*
Deacon	Deacon	*1835–1840*
Dears.	Dearsley, Crown Cases	*1852–1856*
Dears. & B.	Dearsley and Bell	*1856–1858*
Den.	Denison	*1844–1852*
Dick	Dickens	*1559–1792*
Dillon	Dillon's United States Circuit Court Reports	
Doug.	Douglas	*1778–1785*
Dow	Dow	*1812–1818*
Dow & Cl.	Dow and Clark	*1827–1831*
Dowl.	Dowling, Practice Cases	*1830–1841*
Dowl. & N.S.	Dowling, Practice Cases, New Series	*1841–1843*
Dowl. & L.	Dowling and Lowndes	*1843–1849*
Dr. & Sm.	Drewry and Smale	*1859–1865*
Dr. & Wal.	Drury and Walsh	*1837–1841*
Dr. & War.	Drury and Warren	*1841–1843*
Drew.	Drewry	*1852–1859*
Dru.	Drury, temp. Sugden	*1843–1844*
Durnford & East	See T.R.	
Dwar.	Dwarris on Statutes	
Dyer. or Dy.	Dyer	*1513–1582*

E

E.B. & E.	Ellis, Blackburn and Ellis	*1858*
E. & B.	Ellis and Blackburn	*1852–1858*
E.C.J.	Court of Justice of the European Communities	
E.C.R.	European Court Reports	*1975–*
E. & E.	Ellis and Ellis	*1858–1861*
E.G.	Estates Gazette	
E.H.R.R.	European Human Rights Reports	*1979–*
East	East	*1800–1812*
East P.C.	East's Pleas of the Crown	
Eden	Eden	*1757–1766*
Elph.	Elphinstone, Norton and Clark on the Interpretation of Deeds	
Encyc.	Encyclopaedia of the Laws of England	
Eq. Cas. Ab.	Equity Cases Abridged	*1677–1744*
Eq. Rep.	Equity Reports	*1853–1855*
Esp.	Espinasse	*1793–1810*
Ex.	Exchequer Reports	*1847–1856*
Ex. C.R. (preceded by date)	Canada Law Reports, Exchequer	*1923–*
Ex. D.	Law Reports, Exchequer Division	*1875–1880*

F

F.L.R.	Federal Law Reports (Australia)	*1960–*
F.L.R.	Family Law Reports	*1980–*
F.N.B.	Fitz–Herbert, Natura Brevium	
F.S.R.	Fleet Street Reports of Patent Cases	*1963–*
F. & F.	Foster and Finlason	*1856–1867*
Fam. (preceded by date)	Law Reports, Family Division	*1972–*
Fam. Law	Family Law	*1970–*
Farwell	Farwell on Powers	
Fawcett	Fawcett on Landlord and Tenant	
Fearne Cont. Rem.	Fearne on Contingent Remainders and Devises	
Fed. Rep.	Federal Reporter	
Finch	Finch, Heneage	*1673–1680*
Fisher	Fisher on Mortgages	
Florida	Florida Reports	
Fon. B.C.	Fonblanque, Bankruptcy Cases	*1849–1852*
Forrest	Forrest's Exchequer Reports	*1800–1801*

Fort.	Fortescue	*1695–1738*
Foster	Foster's Crown Law Cases	*1708–1760*
Fox & Smith	Fox and Smith	*1822–1824*
Fox Pat. C.	Fox's Patent Cases (Canada)	*1940–*
Fry	Fry on Specific Performance of Con-tracts	

G

G. & D.	Gale & Davison	*1841–1843*
Gale	Gale on Easements	
Gallison	Gallison's United States Circuit Court Reports	
Georgie	Georgie Reports	
Giff.	Giffard	*1857–1865*
Gilb. Eq. Rep.	Gilbert's Equity Reports	*1706–1727*
Godb.	Godbolt	*1575–1642*
Goddard	Goddard on Easements	
Godefroi	Godefroi on Trusts and Trustees	
Goodeve	Goodeve on Real Property	
Gould.	Gouldsborough	*1586–1602*
Gow	Gow	*1818–1820*
Gray	Gray's Massachusetts Reports	

H

H.Bl.	Henry Blackstone	*1788–1796*
H.L.	House of Lords	
H.L. Cas.	House of Lords Cases	*1847–1866*
H.L.R.	Housing Law Reports	*1982–*
H. & C.	Hurlstone and Coltman	*1862–1866*
H. & M.	Hemming and Miller	*1862–1865*
H. & N.	Hurlstone and Norman	*1856–1862*
H. & P.	Hopwood and Philbrick	*1863–1867*
H. & R.	Harrison and Rutherford	*1865–1866*
H. & Tw.	Hall and Twells	*1849–1850*
Hagg. Adm.	Haggard, Admiralty Cases	*1822–1838*
Hagg. Con.	Haggard, Consistory Cases	*1789–1802*
Hagg. Ecc.	Haggard, Ecclesiastical Cases	*1827–1833*
Hale P.C.	Hale's Please of the Crown	
Hamilton	Hamilton on Company Law	
Hard.	Hardres	*1655–1660*
Hare	Hare	*1841–1853*
Hawk.	Hawkins on the Construction of Wills	
Hawk. P.C.	Hawkins' Pleas of the Crown	
Hayes	Hayes	*1830–1832*

Hetley	Hetley	*1627–1631*
Hill	Hill's New York Reports	
Hob.	Hobart	*1603–1625*
Hodges	Hodges	*1835–1837*
Hogan	Hogan	*1816–1834*
Holt	Holt	*1688–1710*
Holt N.P.	Holt, Nisi Prius Cases	*1815–1817*
Hop. & Colt.	Hopwood and Coltman	*1868–1878*
Hud. & Bro.	Hudson and Brooke	*1827–1831*
Hudson	Hudson on Building Contracts	
Hump.	Humphrey's Tennessee Reports	

I

I.C.R.	Industrial Case Reports	*1972–*
I.L.R.	Insurance Law Reporter	*1933–*
I.L.T.R.	Irish Law Times Reports	*1967–*
I.R. (preceded by date)	Irish Reports	*1893–*
I.R.L.R.	Industrial Relations Law Reports	*1972–*
I.T.R.	Industrial Tribunal Reports	
Ibid., ib.	Same case	
Ill.	Illinois Reports	
Imm.A.R.	Immigration Appeal Reports	*1970–*
Inst.	Coke's Institutes	
Iowa	Iowa Reports	
Ir.	Ireland	
Ir. Ch. R.	Irish Chancery Reports	*1850–1866*
I.C.L.R.	Irish Common Law Reports	*1850–1866*
Ir. Eq. R.	Irish Equity Reports	*1838–1850*
Ir. Jur. Rep.	Irish Jurist Reports	*1935–*
Ir.L.R.	Irish Law Reports	*1838–1850*
Ir.R. (preceded by date)	Irish Reports	*1893–*
Ir. Rep. C.L.	Irish Reports, Common Law	*1867–1877*
Ir. Rep. Eq.	Irish Reports, Equity	*1867–1877*

J

J.C.	Justiciary Cases (Scotland)	*1916–*
J. and JJ.	Justice, Justices	
J.P.	Justice of the Peace	*1837–*
J.P.J.	Justice of the Peace Journal	*1837–*
J.P.L. of J.P.P.L.	Journal of Planning and Property Law	*1948–*
J. & H.	Johnson and Hemming	*1859–1862*
J. & La. T.	Jones and La Touche	*1844–1846*

Jac.	Jacob	*1821–1822*
Jac. & W.	Jacob and Walker	*1819–1821*
Jacob	Jacob's Law Dictionary "enlarged and improved" by Tomlins and brought by him "to the end of the reign of our late venerated Sovereign George the Third", 3rd. quarto ed. Sometimes this book is cited as Tomlins, or Tomlins Law Dict.	
Jarm.	Jarman on Wills	
Jebb & B.	Jebb and Bourke	*1841–1842*
Jebb & Sy.	Jebb and Symes	*1838–1841*
Jo. T.	Jones, T.	
1667–1684		
Jo. W.	Jones, William	*1620–1640*
Johns. N.Y.	Johnson's New York Reports	
Johns.	Johnson	*1858–1860*
Johns. Cas.	Johnson's New York Cases	
Johnson	Johnson's Maryland Reports	
Jones & Carey	Jones and Carey	*1838–1839*
Jur.	Jurist	*1837–1854*
Jur. N.S.	Jurist, New Series	*1854–1866*
Juta	Juta's Cape Colony Reports	

K

K.B. (preceded by date)	Law Reports, King's Bench, see now Q.B.	
1901–1952		
K.I.L.R.	Knights Industrial Law Reports	*1975–*
K.I.R.	Knight's Industrial Reports	*1967–1974*
K. & J.	Kay & Johnson	*1854–1958*
Kay	Kay	*1853–1854*
Keble	Keble	*1661–1679*
Keen	Keen	*1836–1838*
Keilwey	Keilwey, ed. of 1688	*1496–1578*
Kelynge W.	Kelynge, William	*1730–1734*
Keyes	Keye's New York Court of Appeal Reports	
Kiralfy	Kiralfy's Action on the Case	
Knapp P.C.	Knapp's Privy Council Cases	*1829–1836*

L

L.C. or C.	Lord Chancellor	
L.C.J. or C.J.	Lord Chief Justice	
L.G.R.	Local Government Reports	*1902–*
L.G.R.A.	Local Government Reports of Australia	*1956–*

L.J.	Law Journal Newspaper	*1866–1965*
L.J. or L.JJ.	Lord Justice, Lords Justices	
L.J. Adm.	Law Journal, New Series, Admiralty	*1866–1875*
L.J. Bank	Law Journal, New Series, Bankruptcy	*1832–1880*
L.J.C.P.	Law Journal, New Series, Common Pleas (in and from 1876–1880, Common Pleas Division)	*1831–1880*
L.J. Ch.	Law Journal, New Series, Chancery	*1831–1880*
L.J. Ecc.	Law Journal, New Series, Ecclesiastical	*1865–1875*
L.J. Ex.	Law Journal, New Series, Exchequer (in and from 1876–1880, Exchequer Division)	*1831–1880*
L.J.K.B., or Q.B.	Law Journal, New Series, King's, or Queen's, Bench (in and from 1876, Queen's, or King's, Bench Division)	*1831–1946*
L.J.M.C.	Law Journal, New Series, Magistrates' Cases	*1831–1896*
L.J.N.C.	Law Journal Notes of Cases	*1866–1892*
L.J.N.C.C.R.	Law Journal Newspaper County Court Reports	*1934–1947*
L.J.O.S.C.P.	Law Journal, Old Series, Common Pleas	*1822–1831*
L.J.O.S. Ch.	Law Journal, Old Series, Chancery	*1822–1823*
L.J.O.S. Ex.	Law Journal, Old Series, Exchequer	*1830–1831*
L.J.O.S. K.B.	Law Journal, Old Series, King's Bench	*1822–1831*
L.J.O.S. M.C.	Law Journal, Old Series, Magistrates' Cases	*1826–1831*
L.J.P.C.	Law Journal, New Series, Privy Council	*1865–1946*
L.J.P.D. & A.	Law Journal, New Series, Probate, Divorce and Admiralty	*1876–1946*
L.J.P. & M.	Law Journal, New Series, Probate, and Matrimonial	*1858–1859, 1986–1875*
L.J.P.M. & A.	Law Journal, New Series, Probate, Matrimonial and Admiralty	*1860–1865*
L.J.R. (preceded by date)	Law Journal Reports	*1947–1949*
L.M. & P.	Lowndes, Maxwell and Pollock	*1850–1851*
L.Q.R.	Law Quarterly Review	*1885–*

L.R.A. & E.	Law Reports, Admiralty and Ecclesiastical	*1865–1875*
L.R.C.C.R.	Law Reports, Crown Cases Reserved	*1865–1875*
L.R.C.P.	Law Reports, Common Pleas	*1865–1875*
L.R. Eq.	Law Reports, Equity	*1865–1875*
L.R. Ex.	Law Reports, Exchequer	*1865–1875*
L.R.H.L.	Law Reports, House of Lords, English and Irish Appeals	*1866–1875*
L.R. Ind. App.	Law Reports, Indian Appeals	*1873–*
L.R. Ir.	Law Reports, Ireland	*1878–1893*
L.R.P.C.	Law Reports, Privy Council	*1865–1875*
L.R.P. & D.	Law Reports, Probate and Divorce	*1865–1875*
L.R.Q.B.	Law Reports, Queen's Bench	*1865–1875*
L.R.R.P.	Law Reports, Restrictive Practices Cases	*1958–*
L.R. Sc. & D. App.	Law Reports, Scottish and Divorce Appeals See also App. Cas.; Ch. D.; Ch.; C.P.D.; Ex. D.; P.D.; Q.B.D.	*1866–1875*
L.T.	Law Times Reports, New Series	*1859–1947*
L.T.J.	Law Times Journal	*1843–1965*
L.T.O.S.	Law Times Reports, Old Series	*1843–1859*
L. & C.	Leigh and Cave	*1861–1865*
L. & G. t. Plunk.	Lloyd and Goold, temp. Plunkett	*1833–1839*
L. & G. t. Sug.	Lloyd and Goold, temp. Sugden	*1835*
Latch	Latch	*1624–1627*
Lea	Lea's Tennessee Reports	
Leach	Leach. Crown Cases	*1730–1814*
Leake	Leake on Contracts	
Lee Ecc.	Lee, Ecclesiastical Cases	*1752–1758*
Leon.	Leonard	*1540–1615*
Lev.	Levinz	*1660–1697*
Lewin	Lewin on Trusts	
Lewin C.C.	Lewin, Crown Cases	*1822–1833*
Lindley Comp.	Lindley on Companies	
Lindley P.	Lindley on Partnership	
Litt.	Littleton's Tenures, the version used being that in the edition of Co. Litt. here used	
Litt. Rep.	Littleton	*1626–1632*
Ll. L. Rep.	Lloyd's List Reports	*1919–1950*
Ll. P.C.	Lloyd's Prize Cases	*1940–*

Lloyd's Rep. (preceded by date)	Lloyd's List Reports	*1951–*
Lofft	Lofft	*1772–1774*
Long. & Town.	Longfield and Townsend	*1841–1842*
Lowndes & Maxwell	See Bail C.C.	
Lush.	Lushington	*1859–1862*
Lutw.	Lutwyche, Registration Cases	*1843–1853*
Lutw. E.	Lutwyche, Edward	*1683–1704*

M

M.P.R.	Maritime Provinces Reports	*1930–*
M.R.	Master of the Rolls	
M. & G.	Manning and Granger	*1840–1844*
M. & R.	Manning and Ryland	*1827–1830*
M. & S.	Maude and Selwyn	*1813–1817*
M. & W.	Meeson & Welsby	*1836–1847*
McL.	McLean's United States Circuit Court Reports	
Mac. & G.	Macnaughten and Gordon	*1849–1852*
Macq.	Macqueen, Scottish Appeals	*1851–1865*
MacS.	MacSweeney on Mines, Quarries and Minerals	
Mad.	Maddock	*1815–1822*
Maine	Maine Reports	
Manson	Manson's Bankruptcy and Winding-up Cases	*1894–1914*
Manwood	Manwood's Forest Laws	
Mar. Cas.	Maritime Cases by Crockford and Cox	*1860–1871*
Marsh.	Marshall	*1813–1816*
Mass.	Massachusetts Reports	
Maude & P.	Maude and Pollock on Merchant Shipping	
Maxwell	Maxwell on the Interpretation of Statutes	
M'Cle.	M'Cleland	*1824*
M'Cle. & Y.	M'Cleland and Younge	*1824–1825*
Megarry	Megarry, The Rent Acts	
Minn.	Minnesota Reports	
Miss.	Mississippi Reports	
Mo.	Missouri Reports	
Mod.	Modern	*1669–1732*
Mod. L.R.	Modern Law Review	*1937–*
Moll.	Molloy	*1827–1828*
Mont.	Montagu	*1829–1832*

Mont. & Ayr.	Montagu and Ayrton	*1833–1838*
Mont. & B.	Montagu and Bligh	*1832–1833*
Mont. & Chitt.	Montagu and Chitty	*1838–1840*
Mont. D. & D.	Montagu, Deacon and De Gex	*1840–1841*
Mont. & M'A	Montague and Macarthur	*1826–1830*
Moo. & M.	Moody and Malkin	*1826–1830*
Moo. & R.	Moody and Robinson	*1830–1844*
Moody	Moody's Crown Cases	*1824–1844*
Moore	Moore, Francis	*1512–1621*
Moore C.P.	Moore, J.B., Common Pleas and Exchequer Chamber Cases	*1817–1827*
Moore Ind. App.	Moore, Indian Appeals	*1836–1872*
Moore P.C.	Moore, Privy Council Appeals	*1836–1862*
Moore P.C.N.S.	Moore, Privy Council Appeals, New Series	*1862–1873*
Moore & P.	Moore and Payne	*1827–1831*
Moore & S.	Moore and Scott	*1831–1834*
Morr.	Morrell, Bankruptcy Cases	*1884–1893*
Moseley	Moseley	*1726–1730*
My. & C.	Mylne and Craig	*1835–1841*
My. & K.	Mylne and Keen	*1832–1835*

N

n.	Note	
N. Hamp.	New Hampshire Reports	
N.I. (preceded by date)	Northern Ireland; Northern Ireland Reports	*1925–*
N.I.L.R.	Northern Ireland Law Reports	*1925–*
N.L.J.	New Law Journal	
N.R.	New Reports	*1862–1865*
N.S.W.R.	New South Wales Reports	*1901–*
N.Y.	New York Reports	
N.Z.L.R.	New Zealand Law Reports	*1883–*
N. & M.	Neville and Manning	*1832–1836*
N. & P.	Neville and Perry	*1836–1838*
N. & P.E.I.R.	Newfoundland and Prince Edward Island Reports	*1970–*
Newb.	Newberry's United States Admiralty Reports	
Nolan	Nolan on the Poor Laws	
Noy	Noy	*1559–1649*

O

O.	Order	
O.L.R.	Ontario Law Reports	*1901–1930*

O.R.	Ontario Reports	*1823–1900*
O.R. (preceded by date)	Ontario Reports	*1931–*
O'M. & H.	O'Malley and Hardcastle	*1869–1934*
Odgers	Odgers on Libel and Slander	
Ohio	Ohio Reports	
Ohio St.	Ohio State Reports	
Ord.	Order	
Orl. Bridg.	Orlando Bridgman	*1660–1667*
Owen	Owen	*1556–1615*

P

P. (preceded by date)	Law Reports, Probate Admiralty and Divorce	*1890–*
P.C.	Privy Council	
P.D.	Law Reports, Probate Divorce and Admiralty Division (*Note.* In and since 1891 these reports are cited by the year, e.g. [1891] P.)	*1875–1890*
P. Wms.	Peere Williams	*1695–1735*
P. & C.R.	Property (previously Planning) and Compensation Reports	*1950–*
P. & D.	Perry and Davison	*1838–1841*
Palm.	Palmer	*1619–1621*
Palmer Co. Pre.	Palmer's Company Precedents	
Para.	Paragraph	
Park	Park on Marine Insurance	
Parker	Parker	*1743–1767*
Pat. Cas. (see R.P.C.)	Patent Cases, by Cutler	*1884–*
Paterson	Paterson's Scottish Appeals	*1851–1873*
Peake	Peake	*1790–1812*
Peake Add. Cas.	Peake, Additional Cases	*1795–1812*
Penn St.	Pennsylvania State Reports	
Phil. Ecc.	Phillimore	*1809–1821*
Phil. Ecc. Law	Phillimore's Ecclesiastical Law	
Phill.	Phillips	*1841–1849*
Pickering	Pickering's Massachusetts Reports	
Platt	Platt on Leases	
Platt Cov.	Platt on Covenants	
Plowd.	Plowden	*1550–1580*
Poll.	Pollexfen	*1660–1685*
Pop.	Popham	*1592–1627*

| Pr. Ch. | Precedents in Chancery, Finch | *1689–1722* |
| Price | Price | *1814–1824* |

Q

Q.B.	Queen's Bench Reports	*1841–1852*
Q.B. (preceded by date)	Law Reports, Queen's Bench	*1891–1901, 1952–*
Q.B.D.	Law Reports, Queen's Bench Division	*1875–1890*
Q.C.L.L.R.	Queensland Crown Lands Law Reports	*1859–*
Q.J.P.R.	Queensland Justice of the Peace Reports	*1907–*
Q.L.R.	Queensland Law Reporter	*1902–1972*
Q.S.	Quarter Sessions	
Q.S.R.	Queensland State Reports	*1902–1957*
Q.W.N.	Queensland Weekly Notes	*1908–*
Qd. R.	Queensland Reports	*1958–*
Que. C.A. (preceded by date)	Quebec Official Reports, Court of Appeal	*1970–*
Que. S.C. (preceded by date)	Quebec Official Reports, Superior Court	*1892*

R

R., r.	Rule	
R.A.	Rating Appeals	*1963–*
R.P.C.	Reports of Patent, Design, and Trade Mark Cases	*1884–*
R.R.C.	Ryde's Rating Cases	*1956–1976*
R.S.A.	Revised Statutes of Alberta	
R.S.C.	Rules of the Supreme Court	
R.S.C.	Revised Statutes of Canada	
R.S.N.S.	Revised Statutes of Nova Scotia	
R.S.O.	Revised Statutes of Ontario	
R.S.P.E.I.	Revised Statutes of Prince Edward Island	
R.S.S.	Revised Statutes of Saskatchewan	
R.T.R.	Road Traffic Reports	*1970–*
R.V.R.	Rating and Valuation Reporter	*1961–*
R. & I.T.	Rating and Income Tax	*1924–*
Raym. Ld.	Lord Raymond	*1694–1732*
Raym. T.	T. Raymond	*1660–1684*
Redman	Redman on Landlord and Tenant	

Reed	Reed on Bills of Sale	
reg.	Regulation	
Rep.	Coke's Reports	*1572–1617*
Rettie	The same as Session Cases, Scottish, 4th series	*1873–1898*
Rice	Rice's South Carolina Reports	
Rob. C.	Robinson, Christopher	*1798–1808*
Rob. Ecc.	Robertson, Ecclesiastical Cases	*1844–1853*
Rob. W.	Robinson, William	*1838–1850*
Robson	Robson on Bankruptcy	
Robt. N.Y.	Robertson's New York Superior Court Reports	
Rogers	Rogers on Elections	
Rol. Ab.	Rolle's Abridgment	
Rolle	Rolle	*1614–1625*
Rop.	Roper on Legacies	
Rosc. Cr.	Roscoe's Digest of the Law of Evidence in Criminal Cases	
Rosc. N.P.	Roscoe's Digest of the Law of Evidence *Nisi Prius*	
Rose	Rose	*1810–1816*
Russ.	Russell	*1823–1829*
Russ. Cr.	Russell on Crimes and Misdemeanours	
Russ. & My.	Russell and Mylne	*1829–1833*
Russ. & Ry.	Russell and Ryan	*1800–1823*
Ry. Cas.	Railway and Canal Cases	*1835–1854*
Ry. & Can. Traffic Cases	Railway and Canal Traffic Cases: cp. B. & Macn. (see Traffic Cas.)	*1855–1950*
Ry. & Moo.	Ryan and Moody	*1823–1826*

S

s.	Section (of Act of Parliament)	
S. or Scot.	Scotland	
S.A.I.R.	South Australian Industrial Reports	*1912–*
S.A.L.R.	South African Law Reports	*1947–*
S.A.S.R.	South Australian State Reports	*1921–*
S.C.	Session Cases (New Series)	*1906–*
S.C.(J.)	Session Cases (High Court of Justiciary)	*1873–1916*
S.C.(H.L.)	Session Cases (House of Lords)	*1852–*
S.C.R.	Canada Law Reports (Supreme Court)	*1923–*
S.I.	Statutory Instruments	
S.J.	Solicitors' Journal	*1856–*

S.L.C.R.	Scottish Land Court Reports	*1913–*
S.L.R.	Scottish Law Reporter	*1865–1924*
S.L.T.	Scots Law Times	*1893–*
S.R. & O.	Statutory Rules and Orders	
S.R. (N.S.W.)	State Reports (New South Wales)	*1901–*
S.T.C.	Simon's Tax Cases	*1973–*
Salk.	Salkeld	*1689–1712*
Saund.	Saunders (see Wms. Saund.)	*1666–1672*
Savile	Savile	*1580–1594*
Sayer	Sayer	*1751–1756*
Sc.	Scott	*1834–1840*
Sc. L.R.	Scottish Law Reporter	*1865–1924*
Sc. N.R.	Scott, New Reports	*1840–1845*
Sch., Sched.	Schedule	
Sch. & Lef.	Schoales and Lefroy	*1802–1807*
Sched.	Schedule	
Scriven	Scriven, Law of Copyholds	
Scrutton	Scrutton on Charter-parties and Bills of Lading	
Selwyn N.P.	Selwyn's *Nisi Prius*	
Sess. Cas. 4th Ser.	Sessions Cases, Scottish, 4th Series	*1874–1898*
Seton	Seton on Decrees	
Sh. Ct. Rep.	Sheriff Court Reports (S.)	*1885–*
Show.	Shower	*1678–1694*
Sid.	Siderfin	*1657–1670*
Sim.	Simons	*1826–1852*
Sim. N.S.	Simons, New Series	*1850–1852*
Sim. & St.	Simons & Stuart	*1822–1826*
Skinner	Skinner	*1681–1697*
Sm. & G.	Smale & Giffard	*1852–1858*
Sm. L.C.	Smith's Leading Cases	
Smythe	Smythe	*1839–1840*
Sneed	Sneed's Tennessee Reports	
Spelm.	Spelman's Glossarium Archaiologicum	
Spinks	Spinks, Ecclesiastical and Admiralty	*1853–1855*
Staf. Def.	Statutory definition, or definitions	
Starkie	Starkie	*1815–1823*
Steph. Cr.	Stephen's Digest of the Criminal Law	
Stone	Stone's Justices' Manual	
Story	Story on Equitable Jurisprudence	
St. R. Qd.	Queensland State Reports	*1902–*
Stra.	Strange	*1715–1748*

Sty. or Style	Style	*1646–1655*
Sug. Pow.	Sugden on Powers	
Sug. Prop.	Sugden on the Law of Property as administered by the House of Lords	
Sug. V. & P.	Sugden on Vendors and Purchasers	
Sumner	Sumner's United States Circuit Court Reports	
Sup. Ct. Pr.	Supreme Court Practice	
Sutton	Sutton on Personal Actions at Common Law	
Sw. & Tr.	Swabey and Tristam	*1858–1865*
Swabey	Swabey	*1855–1859*
Swanst.	Swanston	*1818–1819*

T

T.C.	Tax Cases	*1875–*
T.C. Leaflet	Tax Cases Leaflets	*1938–*
T.L.R.	Times Law Reports	*1884–1950*
T.L.R. (preceded by date)	Times Law Reports	*1951–*
T.R.	Term Reports, same as Durnford and East	*1785–1800*
T.R.	Taxation Reports	*1939–*
T. & M.	Temple and Mews, Criminal Cases	*1848–1851*
T. & R.	Turner and Russell	*1822–1825*
Tas. S.R.	Tasmanian State Reports	*1941–*
Taunt.	Taunton	*1807–1819*
Tax Cas.	Tax Cases	*1875–*
Termes de la Ley	Termes de la Ley — the edition used being that published in London and "printed by Jo. Beale & Ric. Hearne for the benefit of all that are studious in the Common Laws of this Realme, 1641"; "a book of great antiquity and accuracy" (*per* Bayley J., 5 B. & C. 229). If the word is not found in the edition mentioned, then refer to that of 1721	
Texas	Texas Reports	
Theobald	Theobald on Wills	
Tomlins	See Jacob	
Touch	The Touch-Stone, commonly cited as Shep. Touch	
Tr.L.	Trading Law	
Traff. Cas.	Railway, Canal and Road Traffic Cases	*1855–1950*

Tudor Char. Trusts	Tudor on Charitable Trusts	
Tudor's L.C.M.L.	Tudor's Leading Cases on Mercantile Law	
Tudor's L.C.R.P.	Tudor's Leading Cases in Real Property	
Tyr.	Tyrwhitt	*1830–1835*
Tyr. & G.	Tyrwhitt and Granger	*1835–1836*

U

U.S.	United States Supreme Court Reports	
U.S. Dig	United States Digest	

V

v.	Versus	
V.A.T.T.R.	Value Added Tax Tribunal Reports	*1973–*
V.L.R.	Victorian Law Reports	*1875–1956*
V.R.	Victorian Reports	*1957–*
V. & B.	Versey and Beames	*1812–1814*
Vaizey	Vaizey on Settlements	
Vaugh.	Vaughan	*1665–1674*
Ventr.	Ventris	*1668–1684*
Vern.	Vernon	*1681–1719*
Vern. & S.	Vernon and Scriven	*1786–1788*
Ves.	Vesey, junior	*1754–1817*
Ves. sen.	Vesey, senior	*1746–1755*
Vin. Ab.	Viner's Abridgment	

W

W.A.L.R.	West Australian Law Reports	*1898–1959*
W.A.R.	Wester Australian Reports	*1960–*
W. Bl.	William Blackstone	*1746–1780*
W.C.R.	Workers Compensation Reports, New South Wales	*1926–*
W.I.R.	West Indian Reports	
W.L.R. (preceded by date)	Weekly Law Reports	*1953–*
W.N. (preceded by date)	Law Reports, Weekly Notes	*1866–1952*
W.N. (N.S.W.)	Weekly Notes (New South Wales)	*1884–*

W.R.	Weekly Reporter	*1852–1906*
W.W.R.	Western Weekly Reports	*1912–*
W. & D.	Wolferstan and Dew's Election Cases	*1856–1858*
Wallace, or Wall.	Wallace's United States Supreme Court Reports	
Watson Eq.	Watson's Practical Compendium of Equity	
Webster	Webster, Patent Cases	*1601–1855*
Wend.	Wendell's New York Reports	
Wheaton	Wheaton's United States Supreme Court Reports	
White and Tudor	White & Tudor's Leading Cases in Equity	
Wight.	Wightwick	*1810–1811*
Wilberforce	Wilberforce on Statute Law	
Willes	Willes	*1737–1758*
Wils. Ch.	Wilson's Chancery Reports	*1818–1819*
Wils. Ex.	Wilson's Exchequer Reports	*1805–1817*
Wils. K.B.	Wilson's King's Bench Reports	*1742–1774*
Wilson & Shaw	Wilson and Shaw's Scottish Appeals	*1825–1834*
Winch	Winch	*1621–1625*
Wis.	Wisconsin Reports	
Wms. Bank.	Williams on Bankruptcy	
Wms. Exs.	Williams on Executors and Administrators	
Wms. P.P.	Williams on Personal Property	
Wms. R.P.	Williams on Real Property	
Wms. Saund.	Saunders' Reports, with notes by Williams	*1666–1672*
Wms. & Bruce	Williams and Bruce's Admiralty Practice	
Wood	Wood on Mercantile Agreements	
Wood	Wood, Tithe Cases	*1650–1798*
Woodf.	Woodfall on Landlord and Tenant	

Y

Y.B.	Year Books of Reports of Cases	*1307–1537*
Y. & C. Ch.	Younge and Collier, Chancery Cases	*1841–1843*
Y. & C. Ex.	Younge and Collier, Exchequer Cases	*1834–1842*
Y. & J.	Yannge and Jervis	*1826–1830*

RECENT CASES OF PARTICULAR SIGNIFICANCE

Each cumulative supplement to the Sixth Edition will include a short introductory article bringing together and expounding some of the new entries in the year's supplement which are likely to be of particular interest.

Cross-contextual influence of statutory definitions

From its earliest days *Stroud* has always included a number of statutory definitions despite being described as a judicial dictionary. Over the last eight or nine years, in particular, I have tried to strengthen and broaden the statutory material included. The principal justification for this is that statutory definitions in one context are likely not only to be of use to lawyers drafting contracts and other documents in that and other contexts but are also likely to influence the decisions of courts, again in that and other contexts.

A striking example of this is *Parkinson v. St. James and Seacroft University Hospital NHS Trust* [2001] 3 All E.R. 97, CA where Lord Justice Hale was looking for a "solution to the problem of degree: how disabled does a child have to be for the parents to be able to make a claim?" She concluded that she could do no better than borrow a statutory definition of disability from another context, section 17 of the Children Act 1989. She did this not only because the same or a similar definition is found in a number of legislative contexts but also because "local social services authorities are used to operating it".

Construction of expressions which change meaning over time

A question with which all readers of statutes will be familiar is that of how to construe an expression which has changed its meaning since the time when the statute in which it appears was enacted.

As with all questions of statutory interpretation, the correct approach depends not on the application of a fixed doctrine but on determining what Parliament can best be taken to have meant in the particular context. Sometimes the courts will take the view that Parliament must have intended to use an expression in an ambulatory way, encompassing not only a class as at the time of enactment but also anything that might come to fall within that class in the future. This will, of course, be of particular importance when dealing with a class which refers to or depends upon technology.

So, for example, in *Victor Chandler International v. Customs and Excise Commissioners* [2000] 2 All E.R. 315, the Court of Appeal concluded that although when enacting a provision about advertisements in 1952 Parliament could not have contemplated the means by which advertisements can now be distributed electronically, in order to prevent the provision from being undermined it was necessary and appropriate to give the expression "advertisement" an "always speaking" or ambulatory construction to take account of developments since the provision was originally enacted. This breadth of construction is particularly significant given that the provision in question created a criminal offence.

Ordinary versus technical meanings

It is always comforting for those drafting legal documents to know that if they use a word which has an ordinary meaning obvious to and well-understood by ordinary people, the courts will require very good reason to depart from that plain meaning and ascribe a technical meaning to the word in a particular context.

For recent examples of cases in which the courts resisted temptation to depart from the ordinary meaning of a term see: *Anyanwu v. South Bank Students' Union* [2000] 1 All E.R. 1 C.A. ("aids") and *A. E. Beckett & Sons v. Midland Electricity plc* [2001] 1 W.L.R. 291 C.A. ("economic loss").

Pepper v. Hart

For whatever reason, *Pepper v. Hart* did not produce the major change of climate in statutory interpretation which some early commentators predicted. The courts have generally appeared cautious in their recourse to Parliamentary materials, and their admission frequently seems to have had little or no effect on the outcome of the case.

But there is a steady trickle of cases in which the new freedom to have recourse to Parliamentary materials seems to have been helpful to the courts in divining the legislative intent.

So, for example, faced with the question whether the expression "economic loss" in section 21 of the Electricity Act 1989 (c. 29) was intended to have the extended technical meaning which it has acquired in the law of tort, the Court of Appeal was able to conclude that this was not Parliament's intention, relying on clear ministerial statements recorded in *Hansard* in reliance on the rule in *Pepper v. Hart* — see *A. E. Beckett & Sons v. Midland Electricity plc* [2001] 1 W.L.R. 291 C.A.

Purposive construction

It is well established that the courts will sometimes feel obliged to do violence to the literal meaning of an expression in a legal document in order to give effect to what is plainly the intended meaning given the purpose of the document.

A recent example of this is the decision of the Divisional Court in *Talbot v. Director of Public Prosecutions* [2000] 1 W.L.R. 1102 Q.B.D. where the expression "enclosed area" in section 4 of the Vagrancy Act 1824 was held not to include a room in a building. Although in a literal sense a room is by definition an enclosed area, it is beyond doubt that in the context of the 1824 Act the expression is used as a natural colloquial expression whose ordinary meaning is clearly intended to exclude a room.

A particularly interesting recent example is the decision of the House of Lords in *Birmingham City Council v. Oakley* [2000] 3 W.L.R. 1936 H.L. in which the majority felt bound to have regarded to the history and social purpose of the legislation in order to determine how wide a construction to give to the — potentially very wide — expression "state of the premises". (For a related case see the entry in this supplement on *State (of Premises)*.)

Any

"Any" may be the most difficult word to use or construe in a legal document. A large part of the problem is that different people use it in very different ways. Some people use it almost in routine substitution for the indefinite article. Other people use it extremely sparingly.

A legal document which generally relies on the indefinite article can presumably expect the courts to give particular meaning to "any" on the rare occasions on which it is used. Equally, the more "any" is used in cases where "a" would have done the same job, the less the courts are likely to wish to assume that "any" means "any and every" in a context where the point is arguable.

In *Re Proulx; R. v. Bow Street Magistrates' Court, ex parte Proulx* [2001] All E.R. 57 Q.B.D. D.C. the Divisional Court declined to read "any confession" as meaning "any conceivable confession" in a context where it clearly meant something along the lines of "any confession falling within a particular class already mentioned".

Similarly, the High Court found it necessary to read the words "any land not comprised in the lease" in a lease in a restrictive way, limited to land belonging to the landlord — *Paragon Finance plc v. City of London Real Property Co. Ltd, The Times*, August 20, 2001, Ch.

In particular

There are many occasions when a term in a legal document is sufficiently vague for it to be wise for those responsible for the drafting to give some examples of matters which are specifically intended to be included within the term but which one could not rely on the courts to include on a natural construction of the term. Of course, as soon as one starts to provide a list of examples one runs the risk that the natural construction of the term will be narrowed and that it will be taken as referring either only to the items actually in the list or to a class of things of which those items form examples.

Some time ago it was common for this risk to be avoided by provision to the effect that "Nothing in this [section] shall prejudice the generality of ...]. This is generally thought a little heavy handed these days, although there are occasions on which it seems the most appropriate approach.

A common modern alternative with a considerably lighter touch is simply to say ", in particular," before the list of examples. That does not, of course, ensure that the list will have no narrowing effect on the construction of the general principle at all — that could hardly be expected, and is not achieved even by the "nothing shall prejudice the generality" line, because the mind of the reader cannot but be affected by the list in his contemplation of the general expression.

All this depends on ", in particular" being taken by the courts not to have too limiting an effect. It is therefore reassuring — although not surprising — that the House of Lords in *R. v. City of Westminster Housing Benefit Review Board, ex parte Mehanne* [2001] 2 All E.R. 690 H.L. rejected the suggestion that a statutory instrument which required a local authority to reduce a person's rent by such amount as it considered appropriate "having regard in particular to the cost of suitable alternative accommodation" excluded consideration of factors other than the one particularised.

As to whether a requirement to have particular regard to specified matters required more weight to be given to those matters than others, see the judgment of Sir Andrew Morritt V.-C. (rejecting the notion) in *Ashdown v. Telegraph Group* [2001] 2 All E.R. 370, 383 Ch.

For a related question, the application of the *eiusdem generis* rule to the construction of "and other [matters]" see the entry in this supplement on *Other*.

Criminal versus civil proceedings

Once there was rarely difficulty in knowing whether a matter before the courts was civil or criminal. Recently there has been a proliferation of procedures of hybrid appearance which can make the question difficult. This supplement contains a number of cases on the point as it relates to new kinds of matter: see, in particular, the entries *Civil proceedings*, *Charged with a criminal offence*, *Criminal cause or matter*, *Criminal proceedings*, *Conviction* and *Criminal investigation*.

Statutory headings

An old question familiar to all those who have to construe statutes is to what extent (if any) is it permissible or advisable to have regard to headings of different kinds. The answer varies throughout the decades partly as a reflection of changing practice — particularly Parliamentary practice — in respect of headings and partly reflecting a general trend towards inclination by the courts to look at anything which they think may help them.

In *R. (on the application of Toth) v. Solicitors Disciplinary Tribunal* [2001]

3 All E.R. 180 Q.B.D. Stanley Burnton J. says (paragraph 27) "The heading of part III of the 1994 rules (Solicitors Disciplinary Proceedings Rules 1994) is "General". It does not indicate that the 1994 rules in Part III apply other than generally. It is permissible to have regard to such headings in a statutory instrument".

Why headings in statutory instruments should be different from some or all headings in statutes is not entirely clear. In any event the more the courts come to rely generally on headings in one context the more they are likely to do so in other contexts.

Calculation of periods of time

The calculation of periods of time is one of the most striking contexts in which legal drafting requires a degree of precision which would be not only unnecessary but wholly absurd in ordinary conversation.

The expression "two years" from the end of the bankruptcy would be regarded for almost every purpose as a sufficiently exact expression. And it can happen that even in legal documents a period of time is thought to have been stated sufficiently exactly without it having been expressed whether the day, week, month or year which marks one end of the period is to be included for the purpose of calculating it.

One might think that the point was sufficiently obvious and famous for those drafting contracts and other legal documents to avoid it, and that it would have been settled sufficiently definitively by the courts centuries ago for it to be unnecessary to litigate the occasional oversight. But although there is indeed a respectable set of ancient cases (see, for example, the early parts of the sixth edition's entries on "after" and "from") the point still occasionally emerges in the courts.

Zoan v. Rouamba [2000] 1 W.L.R. 1509, [2000] 2 All E.R. 620, C.A. is notable not so much for any innovation of approach or decision but for the comfortingly predictable way in which the Court of Appeal stuck to the long-established general principles and refused to be deflected by the fact that the context concerned the proper European construction of Community legislation.

The result is that Chadwick L.J.'s judgment in *Zoan* provides both a useful rehearsal of the established rules about the calculation of periods of time and evidence that the judges will be reluctant to disturb these rules, which are based both on long usage and on common sense. In particular, "The usual meaning of the words 'after' or 'from' in the context of reckoning time, as the authorities make clear, is that the day 'after' or 'from' which a period of time is to be reckoned is not included within the period" (para. 34). "Where, however, the period within which the act is to be done is expressed to be a period beginning with a specified day, then it has been held, with equal consistency over the past forty years or thereabouts, that the legislature (or the relevant rule-making body, as the case may be) has shown a clear intention that the specified day must be included in the period" (para. 24).

Communication

The enormous changes in the field of communication technology over recent years raise a number of challenges for the application of traditional legal concepts and for the interpretation of traditional legal phrases. Helpful statutory definitions of aspects of electronic communication are beginning to appear: see, by way of recent example, the Electronic Communications Act 2000 (c. 7), passim, and the Regulation of Investigatory Powers Act 2000 (c. 23), s. 56 (electronic signature). And see also *Morgans v. Director of Public Prosecutions* [2000] 2 All E.R. 522 H.L.

Similarly, statutory definitions of "document" tend to place increasing emphasis on new kinds of methods of information storage. A number are recorded both in the sixth edition itself and in this supplement.

Enactment

It is well known and documented that the word "enactment" can — depending on the context — be used in statute to include kinds of legislation apart from Acts and Measures (although one might think that it is only they which are "enacted", strictly speaking). An interesting development in the increasing potential width of the term is the inclusion of a piece of European legislation: the Court of Appeal decided that a Council Regulation is an enactment for the purposes of section 170(2) of the Customs and Excise Management Act 1979 (fraudulent evasion of prohibition or restriction in respect of goods under an enactment) — *R. v. Sissen* [2001] 1 W.L.R. 902 C.A.

Simple contract debt

Provisions to the effect that a particular sum was to be regarded as if owed by simple contract debt were once common. In recent years they have been included only rarely.

At one stage this provision was required in order to give the county courts jurisdiction in the matter: but they now have statutory jurisdiction to deal with recovery of sums due under statute (see County Courts Act 1984). At another stage in the history of this phrase it had significance in respect of limitation periods: but now the limitation periods for contract and statutory debts are the same.

The phrase recently acquired renewed significance, as a result of the decision of the Court of Appeal in *Agodzo v. Bristol City Council* [1999] 1 W.L.R. 1971 C.A. There the court construed the provision for a sum to be recovered as a "simple contract debt" as enabling the debtor to seek a declaration from a county court that the sum was unreasonable despite the fact that there were no proceedings for recovery, since the recovering public authority had been satisfied by the mortgagee who repossessed the property in respect of which the sum was owing.

Whether this will result in the revival of the use of the provision for sums to be regarded as owing by simple contract debt remains to be seen. But it is probably unlikely. The circumstances of *Agodzo* were, in this respect, very unusual. And there would have been other ways of challenging the council's decision in the courts without reliance on the novel construction given to it by the Court of Appeal.

A

ABOUT.

(1) As a term of approximation.

The inclusion of the word "about" in a contract or other legal document implies the need to be influenced by the facts and circumstances on each occasion. If it were possible to be exact for all cases about the degree of latitude to be allowed, one would expect it to be specified.

The courts will therefore reject an invitation to be prescriptive in deciding one case about what degree of variation would satisfy "about" in another case, even in the same context. See, for example, *Arab Maritime Petroleum Transport Co. v. Luxor Trading Corporation and Geogas Enterprise S.A., The Al Bida* [1987] 1 Lloyd's Rep. 124 (charter providing that a vessel was capable of maintaining "about 15.5 knots" in moderate weather).

That the margin of latitude permitted by "about" can on occasion be considerable is illustrated by the case of *Louis Dreyfus v. Parnaso Cia. Naviera* [1960] 2 Q.B. 49. A charterparty obligation to ship "about 10,400 tons" was satisfied despite a deficiency of 331 tons.

(2) In a temporal context.

For early cases on the degree of latitude implied by "about" in a temporal context see: *Watkinson v. Wilson* 55 S.J. 617 ("about four years"); *Patterson v. Macdonald* 31 Sc. L.R. 517 ("or about that time"); *Meyer v. Sanderson & Co.* 32 T.L.R. 428 ("about six months").

(3) "About to [do something]"

A person is not "about to" do something merely because he has an intention to do it — *R. v. Goodwin* [1944] K.B. 518 ("about to commit" an offence, Prevention of Crimes Act 1871 (c. 112), s. 7). The idea is more that the person is just ready to do the thing in question: see, for example, *Bensten v. Taylor* [1893] 2 Q.B. 274, *per* Esher M.R. (construing "now sailed, or about to sail" in a charterparty).

The entry above replaces the entry in the main work.

ACCIDENT.

An indecent assault committed on a person could be an "accident" within the meaning of article 17 of the Warsaw Convention 1929 Scheduled to the Carriage by Air Act 1961 since it was one of the particular risks inherent in air travel. *Morris v. K.L.M. Royal Dutch Airlines* [2001] 3 All E.R. 126 C.A., [2001] 3 W.L.R. 351 C.A.

For a review of the meaning of the term in connection with entitlement to industrial injuries benefit (in particular, *Chief Adjudication Officer v. Faulds*) see N.L.J., September 15, 2000, pp. 1328–29.

ACCOMMODATION.
Placing students free of charge for periods of short duration in families where they were considered to be equal to the rest of the family did not amount to the provision of accommodation for the purposes of the definition of travel packages in Council Directive 90/314. *Administrative Proceedings Against AFS Intercultural Programs Finland Ry* (Case C-237/97) [2000] 1 C.M.L.R. 845 E.C.J.

ACCOUNTING OFFICER.
For the definition of accounting officer of a government department see the Government Resources and Accounts Act 2000 (c. 20), s. 5(6).

ACTION (IN CONTEXT OF LEGAL PROCEEDINGS).
The term "action" in section 15(1) of the Limitation Act 1980 (c. 58) ("No action shall be brought by any person to recover land ...") does not include either an application to the Land Registry in respect of a caution or legal proceedings in a court which would not result in recovery of possession. *J. A. Pye (Oxford) Ltd v. Graham* [2000] 3 W.L.R. 242 Ch.

ACTION FOUNDED ON TORT.
See TORT.

ADVERTISEMENT.
The phrase "advertisement or other document" in section 9(1)(b) of the Betting and Gaming Duties Act 1981 (c. 63) was to be construed not by reference to the kind of advertisement possible when the Act was passed, but in an ambulatory way. So a form of electronic advertisement which could not have been within the contemplation of the legislature when the Act was passed was nevertheless within the ambit of the phrase as it had effect later. *Victor Chandler International v. Customs and Excise Commissioners* [2000] 2 All E.R. 315. This approach is comparatively new: in earlier times the maxim *contemporanea expositio est optima et fortissima in lege* was applied to produce the opposite result. But it is possible that the old approach will continue to be relied upon in certain kinds of circumstance.

AFFRAY.
Carrying petrol bombs which were neither brandished nor waved might constitute a threat of unlawful violence for the purposes of an affray under section 3(1) of the Public Order Act 1986, but only if the threat were directed at someone at the scene. *I. v. Director of Public Prosecutions* [2001] 2 W.L.R. 765 H.L., [2001] 2 All E.R. 583 H.L. ([2001] UKHL/10).

AFRICAN.
"African", as it is generally used in ordinary speech in England and Wales, does not refer to a group of persons defined by reference to nationality or ethnic or national origins but does describe a "racial group" in so far as it denotes personal characteristics of the blacks of Africa who are a limited

group of people regarded as of common stock and as one of the major divisions of humankind having in common distinct physical features. *R. v. White (Anthony)* [2001] 1 W.L.R. 1352 C.A.

AFTER.
In reckoning periods of time a reference to a period "after" a day normally has the effect of excluding that day from the reckoning. *Zoan v. Rouamba* [2000] 1 W.L.R. 1509 C.A.

AGGREGATE (IN CONTEXT OF MINERALS).
Stat. Def., Finance Act 2001 (c. 9), s. 17(1).

AGREEMENT.
Stat. Def., "includes any arrangement or understanding (whether or not legally enforceable)" (Social Security Contributions and Benefits Act 1992 (c. 4), Sched. 1, para. 3A(4), inserted by Child Support, Pensions and Social Security Act 2000 (c. 19), s. 77(1).

AID.
On its true construction, the verb "aids" in section 33(1) of the Race Relations Act 1976 contemplated a state of affairs in which one party, being a free agent, set out to act or to achieve a result and another party assisted him to do it. That was an ordinary English expression and there was nothing in the social purposes of the legislation to suggest that it should be given any specially extended meaning. *Anyanwu v. South Bank Students' Union* [2000] 1 All E.R. 1 C.A. The House of Lords reversed the finding of the Court of Appeal but purported also to construe "aids" as an ordinary English word bearing no technical or special meaning — [2001] 1 W.L.R. 638 H.L., [2001] 2 All E.R. 353 HL ([2001] UKHL/14). For a case applying *Anyanwu* see *Hallam v. Avery* [2001] 1 W.L.R. 655 H.L. ([2001] UKHL/15).

AID OR ABET.
A classic statement of the concept is found in the words of Hawkins J. in *R. v. Coney* 51 L.J.M.C. 78: "To constitute an aider or abbettor, some active steps must be taken, by word or action, with intent to instigate the principal or principals. Encouragement does not, of necessity, amount to aiding and abetting. It may be intentional or unintentional. A man may unwittingly encourage another in fact by his presence, by misinterpreted gestures, or by his silence or non-interference — or he may encourage intentionally by expressions, gestures, or actions, intended to signify approval. In the latter case he aids and abets; in the former he does not. It is no criminal offence to stand by a mere passive spectator of a crime, even of a murder. Non-interference to prevent a crime is not itself a crime. But the fact that a person was voluntarily and purposely present witnessing the commission of a crime, and offered no opposition to it, though he might reasonably be expected to prevent it, and had the power so to do or at least to express his dissent, might, under some circumstances, afford cogent evidence upon which a jury would

be justified in finding that he wilfully encouraged, and so aided and abetted. But it would be purely a question for the jury whether he did so or not".

Note that a person can sometimes aid and abet by mere non-interference. See *Du Cros. v. Lambourne* [1907] 1 K.B. 40 (owner of a motor car not interfering with person driving it at an improper speed) or *Rubie v. Faulkner* [1940] 1 K.B. 571 (supervisor of learner driver).

See also AID, ABET, COUNSEL OR PROCURE.

AID, ABET, COUNSEL OR PROCURE.
For what this adds to "aid and abet" see *Benford v. Sims* [1898] 2 Q.B. 641 and *Attorney General's Reference (No. 1 of 1975)* [1975] Q.B. 773.

ALTERATION.
Alteration distinguished from partial demolition: see PARTIAL DEMOLITION.

ANNIVERSARY.
A reference to "the first anniversary" of an agreement ought normally to be construed as a reference to one day later than the last day of the period of 12 months including the date of the agreement. *Zoan v. Rouamba* [2000] 1 W.L.R. 1509 C.A.

ANNUITY.
Regular monthly payments of a specific amount made to a claimant's Court of Protection receiver under an agreement for a structured settlement were annuity payments within the meaning of regulation 41(2) of the Income Support (General) Regulations 1987. *Beattie v. Secretary of State for Social Security* [2001] 1 W.L.R. 1404 C.A.

ANY.
The potential ambiguity of this word is illustrated by *Re Proulx*; *R. v. Bow Street Magistrates' Court, ex p. Proulx* [2001] All E.R. 57 Q.B.D. D.C. The courts declined to read "any confession" as meaning "any conceivable confession" in a context where it clearly meant something along the lines of "any confession falling within a particular class already mentioned". Statutes sometimes restrict the apparent breadth of "any" by qualifying it with "such". But it may be preferable to omit it altogether and rely on the indefinite article alone. A statute which generally uses "a" can expect particular significance to be attached by a construing court to the occasional use of "any".

APPARATUS.
Stat. Def., Regulation of Investigatory Powers Act 2000 (c. 23), s. 81(1).

APPROPRIATION.
In section 3(1) of the Theft Act 1968 (c. 60) appropriation is a neutral word comprehending any assumption of an owner's rights. So a gift obtained in

circumstances which suggested unfair pressure or the taking of an unfair advantage could amount to theft. So held the House of Lords (by 3:2) in *R. v. Hinks* [2000] 3 W.L.R. 1590 H.L, [2000] 4 All E.R. 833 H.L.

APPROPRIATION IN AID.

For the meaning of "appropriation in aid" in the context of government accounting, see the Government Resources and Accounts Act 2000 (c. 20), s. 2, which defines the concept for the purpose of the new system, introduced by the Act, of resource budgeting and accounting.

ARTISTIC.

"Work of artistic craftsmanship". For a work to be regarded as a work of artistic craftsmanship it must be possible fairly to say that the author is both a craftsman and an artist. Designs for bedspread and cushion covers did not, therefore, constitute "work of artistic craftsmanship" within section 4(1)(c) of the Copyright, Designs and Patents Act 1988 (c. 48). The samples produced were works of craftsmanship and pleasing to the eye but the result was not sufficiently artistic or creative enough to come within section 4(1)(c). *Vermaat v. Boncrest Limited*, June 23, 2000 T.L.R. Ch.

ASSET.

Stat. Def., "includes any right or interest" (Trustee Act 2000 (c. 29), s. 39(1)).

BADGER SETT.

Section 14 of the Protection of Badgers Act 1992 (c. 51) defines a badger sett as "any structure or place which displays signs indicating current use by a badger". The Divisional Court found that in the context of a penal provision the term badger sett and its statutory definition was to be given a confined meaning. In particular, a badger sett was not to be regarded as including all the area up to and including the surface area above the system of tunnels and chambers. It included the tunnels and chambers themselves and the areas immediately outside the entrance holes to those tunnels and chambers, and it might also apply in other circumstances such as where badgers occupied coverts or disused sheds as a shelter or refuge. *Director of Public Prosecutions v. Green* [2001] 1 W.L.R. 505 Q.B.D.

BANKING INSTRUMENT.

Stat. Def., Postal Services Act 2000 (c. 26), s. 7(5).

BANKRUPTCY.

"Bankruptcy proceedings". For the purposes of Article 16(1) of the Convention on Jurisdiction and the Enforcement of Judgements in Civil and Commercial Matters 1968 (implemented by the Civil Jurisdiction and Judgments Act 1982) bankruptcy proceedings are proceedings in which bankruptcy is the principal subject matter and do not include a property claim brought by a trustee in bankruptcy in respect of a bankrupt's assets vested in him. *Ashurst v. Pollard* [2001] 2 W.L.R. 722 C.A., [2001] 2 All E.R. 75 C.A.

BAREBOAT CHARTER TERMS.

Stat. Def., Finance Act 2000 (c. 17), Sched. 22, para. 143.

BEGINNING WITH.

See *Zoan v. Rouamba* [2000] 1 W.L.R. 1509 C.A., [2000] 2 All E.R. 620 C.A.

BEHAVIOUR.

Stat. Def., "includes action or inaction" (Financial Services and Markets Act 2000 (c. 8), s. 118(10)).

BENEFIT.

Stat. Def., "includes any allowance, payment, credit or loan" (Social Security Administration Act 1992 (c. 5), s. 121DA(5), inserted by Child Support, Pensions and Social Security Act 2000 (c. 19), Sched. 6, para. 8).

BEQUEST.

Stat. Def., "includes any form of testamentary disposition" (Political Parties, Elections and Referendums Act 2000 (c. 41), s. 160).

BET.

"Spread bet", see SPREAD BET.

BET-BROKER.

Stat. Def., Betting and Gaming Duties Act 1981 (c. 63), s. 5C inserted by Finance Act 2001 (c. 9), Sched. 1, para. 1.

BLIND EYE KNOWLEDGE.

A person has blind eye knowledge of the unseaworthiness of a vessel if he has a suspicion or belief that the vessel is unseaworthy and deliberately refrains from making relevant inquiries. *Manifest Shipping Co. Ltd v. Uni-Polaris Shipping Co. Ltd* [2001] 2 W.L.R. 170 H.L., [2001] 1 All E.R. 743 H.L.

BODILY INJURY.

The true construction of the phrase "bodily injury" in article 17 of the Warsaw Convention 1929 scheduled to the Carriage by Air Act 1961 was physical injury, excluding mental injury or distress (other than in consequence of death or physical injury of the claimant or someone related to him). *Morris v. K.L.M. Royal Dutch Airlines* [2001] 3 All E.R. 126 C.A.

BODY.

Stat. Def., including partnership, Financial Services and Markets Act 2000 (c. 8), s. 367(2).

Stat. Def., including group of bodies, partnership or enterprise carried on by one or more persons or bodies and a body which is substantially the same as, or successor to, another body, Government Resources and Accounts Act 2000 (c. 20), s. 17(7).

BONA FIDE.

The phrase bona fide is used in many contexts in each of which it will necessarily have particular connotations. Little assistance is likely to be gained in construing the phrase in one context from its decided meaning in another. For this reason the present work omits a number of old references to the term, particularly as it relates to concepts which no longer have relevance (such as the once crucial question whether a claim of right is bona fide so as to oust jurisdiction of inferior tribunals). Earlier editions of this work will, however, provide ample evidence of the meaning of this phrase in contexts which are no longer of practical utility.

The fundamental meaning in all contexts is something along the lines of "honestly" — see Bramwell L.J. *R. v. Holl*, 7 Q.B.D. 575.

That leads one to question what the term can sensibly mean when applied to inanimate things, incapable of honesty or dishonesty. Even applied to individuals the phrase will sometimes be of doubtful effect.

So, for example, Williams J. in *Atkinson v. Sellers*, 28 L.J.M.C. 13 asserts that "bona fide traveller" in section 1 of the Sale of Beer Act 1854 (c. 79) means no more than "traveller" — for "Can a man be said to be a mala fide traveller? Yet the judge's question is answered in *Penn v. Alexander* [1893] 1 Q.B. 522 where the court held that a person who travelled the prescribed distance of three miles but only for the purpose of obtaining a drink during prohibited hours was not a bona fide traveller. Dishonesty could perhaps be imputed in the sense that the person must have known that the intention of the exemption for travellers was not to require people to travel in order to drink but to permit the provision of drinks to facilitate travelling undertaken for other reasons.

That can be contrasted with "bona fide parishioner" where "I suppose anybody would have a difficulty in defining the difference between a parishioner and a bona fide parishioner. I do not know what the difference is between them" (*per Etherington v. Wilson* 1 Ch. D. 160). It is hard to imagine anybody becoming a parishioner with intent purely to take unfair advantage of some privilege or provision relating to parishioners.

If a general rule can be distilled from these instances it may be that the draftsman who uses bona fide in a legal document must satisfy himself that the relevance of honesty or dishonesty to the action or thing is clear. If it is clearly possible to argue whether there is any relevance or what the relevance is, the draftsman will need to use some other phrase to illustrate the policy (unless, of course, it is preferable or unavoidable to live with the acknowledged uncertainty).

The job once frequently done by the concept of bona fides and mala fides is frequently done today in other ways. For example, the notion of the mala fide exercise of a statutory power where land is taken for a purpose not authorised by Parliament — see *London & North Western Railway v. Westminster* [1904] 1 Ch. 767, reversed on the facts [1905] A.C. 426) — could nowadays probably be approached simply by way of express or implied limitation on vires.

The following relatively recent cases will suffice to give a general flavour of the courts' attitude to bona fides:

Attorney General v. Johnson [1903] 1 K.B. 617 (bona fide sale);

United Dominions Trust v. Kirkwood [1966] 2 Q.B. 431 and *Hafton Properties v. McHugh* (1986) T.C. Leaflet No. 3069 (bona fide banking business);

Baume & C. v. A. H. Moore [1958] Ch. 907 (bona fide use by a person of his name, meaning without intention to deceive or to make use of another's goodwill);

Clark v. I.R.C. [1979] 1 W.L.R. 416 (bona fide commercial reasons);

Parr v. Bolton [1996] 8 C.L. 81 (bona fide use of court process, meaning activity furthering a client's case).

See also IN GOOD FAITH, FAIR AND REASONABLE, and MISTAKE.

The entry above replaces the entry in the main work.

BOOSTER SEAT.
Stat. Def., Value Added Tax Act 1994 (c. 23), Sched. A1, para. 7 inserted by Finance Act 2001 (c. 9), s. 96.

BRIDGE.
Stat. Def., "means a bridge or viaduct and includes the abutments of a bridge" (Transport Act 2000 (c. 38), s. 198).

BURGLARY.
See DOMESTIC BURGLARY.

BUS.
Stat. Def., Transport Act 2000 (c. 38), s. 144(14).

BUSINESS.
For what amounts to the carrying on of a business by a club or association see *Eastbourne Town Radio Cars Association v. Customs and Excise Commissioners* [2001] 2 All E.R. 597 HL ([2001] UKHL/19).

Stat. Defs., Limited Liability Partnerships Act 2000 (c. 12), s. 18) ("includes every trade, profession and occupation"); Transport Act 2000 (c. 38), s. 182(4) (wide definition including government, &c. business).

BYWAY.
The true construction of the definition of byway in section 66(1) of the Wildlife and Countryside Act 1981 (c. 69) is as referring to a type of highway, not only to those which are currently and actually used by the public mainly for the purpose for which footpaths and bridleways are used. *Masters v. Secretary of State for the Environment* [2000] 2 All E.R. 788 Q.B.D, affirmed [2000] 4 All E.R. 458 C.A, [2000] 3 W.L.R. 1894 C.A. Note that *Masters* at first instance was expressly not followed by Kay J. in *Buckland v. Secretary of State for the Environment, Transport and the Regions* [2000] 1 W.L.R. 1949 QBD: he held thatsection 66(1) of the 1981 Act did require evidence of current use of the route in question by the public (although not evidence of vehicular use).

C

CAPACITY.
For a discussion of what is meant by "capacity" to sue (as used in the Civil Practice Rules r. 17.4(4)) see *Haq v. Singh* [2001] 1 W.L.R. 1594 C.A.

CAPITAL EXPENDITURE.
Stat. Def., Capital Allowances Act 2001 (c. 2), ss. 4 and 10.

CAPITAL PAYABLE BY INSTALMENTS.
See ANNUITY.

CAPITAL SUMS.
Stat. Def., Capital Allowances Act 2001 (c. 2), s. 4.

CAR.
Stat. Def., Income and Corporation Taxes Act 1988 (c. 1), Sched. 12AA, para. 3(2) inserted by Finance Act 2001 (c. 9), Sched. 12.

CARE HOME.
See RESIDENTIAL CARE HOME.

CARE WORKER.
Stat. Def., Care Standards Act 2000 (c. 14), s. 80(2).
   See also SOCIAL CARE WORKER.

CASH.
Stat. Def., "includes money in any form" (Trustee Act 2000 (c. 29), s. 3(6)).

CAUSE.
As a description of legal proceedings, "cause" is wider than "action" in that it is apt to describe criminal proceedings. *Bridgewater v. Griffiths* [2000] 1 W.L.R. 524 Q.B.D. *per* Burton J. at 536F.

CHARGE.
Stat. Def., "includes a mortgage (or, in Scotland, a security over property)" (Financial Services and Markets Act 2000 (c. 8), s. 112(15)).

CHARGED WITH A CRIMINAL OFFENCE.
A person is not "charged with a criminal offence" within the meaning of article 6(2) of the European Convention for the Protection of Human Rights and Fundamental Freedoms 1950 (as set out in Schedule 1 to the Human Rights Act 1998 (c. 42)) where an application is made against him for a

confiscation order under the Proceeds of Crime (Scotland) Act 1995 (c. 43). *McIntosh v. Lord Advocate* [2001] 2 All E.R. 638 P.C. [2001] 3 W.L.R. 107 P.C. ([2001] U.K.P.C. D1).

CHARITABLE TRUST.
Stat. Def., Trustee Act 2000 (c. 29), s. 39(1).

CHARITY.
Stat. Def., "means any body of persons or trust established for charitable purposes only" (Finance Act 2000 (c. 17), s. 46(6)).

CHARTER.
See BAREBOAT CHARTER TERMS.

CHIEF EXECUTIVE.
In relation to body corporate, Stat. Def., Financial Services and Markets Act 2000 (c. 8), s. 417(1).

CHILDREN'S CAR SEAT.
Stat. Def., Value Added Tax Act 1994 (c. 23), Sched. A1, para. 7 inserted by Finance Act 2001 (c. 9), s. 96.

CHURCHWARDEN.
Stat. Def., Churchwardens Measure 2001 (No. 1), s. 1.

CIRCUS.
Stat. Def., Dangerous Wild Animals Act 1976 (c. 38), s. 7(4) as amended by the Zoo Licensing Act 1981 (c. 37); definition considered *South Kesteeven District Council v. Mackie* [2000] 1 W.L.R. 1461 C.A. (animals' winter quarters did not count as circus and therefore did not need licence).

CIVIC.
The expression "organisation with aims of a ... civic nature" in article 13A(1)(1) of the Sixth Council Directive on Value Added Tax (77/388/EEC) was not restricted to organisations of an ultruistic nature; provided that it were not profit-making an organisation which aimed to promote and support the proper administration of justice and the early resolution of disputes could fall within the phrase, notwithstanding the fact that it proved activities and benefits for members. *Expert Witness Institute v. Customs and Excise Commissioners* [2001] W.L.R. 1658 Ch.

CIVIL PROCEEDINGS.
With the increasing incidence of "civil penalties" a number of kinds of proceeding which might be thought to have criminal aspects or implications are classified strictly as civil proceedings. So, for example, the civil standard of proof can be applied to applications relating to sex offender orders, which are not criminal proceedings because there is no new charge or finding of

guilt — *B. v. Chief Constable of the Avon and Somerset Constabulary* [2001] 1 All E.R. 562 Q.B.D. D.C., [2001] 1 W.L.R. 340 Q.B.D. D.C. And similarly proceedings for an anti-social behaviour order under section 1 of Crime and Disorder Act 1998 are distinct from criminal proceedings to enforce the order and are not themselves criminal proceedings — *R. (McCann) v. Manchester Crown Court* [2001] 1 W.L.R. 358 Q.B.D. D.C.

See also CHARGED WITH A CRIMINAL OFFENCE, CRIMINAL CAUSE OR MATTER and CRIMINAL PROCEEDINGS.

Stat. Def., "any proceedings in or before any court or tribunal that are not criminal proceedings [as defined]" (Regulation of Investigatory Powers Act 2000 (c. 23), s. 81(1)).

COASTAL LAND.
Stat. Def., Countryside and Rights of Way Act 2000 (c. 37), s. 3(3).

COMMUNICATION.
Stat. Def., Regulation of Investigatory Powers Act 2000 (c. 23), s. 81(1).

CONSENT.
Article 7(1) of First Council Directive (89/104/EEC) on trademarks prevents the proprietor of a trade mark from prohibiting its use in relation to goods put on the market in the European Economic Area by the proprietor "or with his consent". The European Court of Justice held that consent in this context is to be construed as consent to the marketing of each individual item of goods and cannot be inferred from consent given to the marketing of other identical or similar products. *Sebago Inc. v. GB-Unic SA* [2000] 2 W.L.R. 1341 E.C.J.

CONSEQUENTIAL.
Where one thing precedes another, can the first ever be "consequential" to the second? A direction to administrators was a consequential provision within the meaning of section 18(3) of the Insolvency Act 1986 — being something which resulted directly or indirectly from the discharge of an administration order — even though it necessarily took effect before the discharge. *In re UCT (U.K.) Ltd* [2001] 1 W.L.R. 436 Ch.

CONSIGNEE & CONSIGNOR.
As used in the Warsaw Convention scheduled to the Carriage by Air Act 1961 the terms are not limited to the persons named as consignor or consignee in the air waybill but can include principals of those named, whether disclosed or not. *Western Digital Corporation v. British Airways P.L.C.* [2000] 3 W.L.R. 1855 C.A.

CONTRACT.
See SIMPLE CONTRACT DEBT.

CONVICTION.
Stat. Def., including a reference to a finding under section 11(1) of the Powers of Criminal Courts (Sentencing) Act 2000 (c. 6) that the accused did the act charged but requires medical examination: same Act, s. 10(8)(a).

COMMUNICATION.
For discussion of the nature of an electronic communication, see *R. v. Effik* [1994] 3 All E.R. 458 HL and *Morgans v. Director of Public Prosecutions* [2000] 2 All E.R. 522 H.L. See also Stat. Def., Electronic Communications Act 2000 (c. 7), s. 15(1) ("includes a communication comprising sounds or images or both and a communication effecting a payment").
See also ELECTRONIC COMMUNICATION.

COMMUNITY LAW.
The expression "rule of Community law" as used in regulation 13(b) of the General Product Safety Regulations 1994 means a rule created by an organ of the European Communities, such as the Commission or the Court of Justice. It does not include a provision of a domestic statute (whether or not related to a Community obligation). *Caerphilly County Borough Council v. Stripp* [2001] 2 C.M.L.R. 5 Q.B.D.

COMPENSATION ORDER.
Stat. Def., Powers of Criminal Courts (Sentencing) Act 2000 (c. 6), s. 130.

CONDUCT.
Stat. Def., "includes acts, omissions and statements" (Social Security Administration Act 1992 (c. 5), s. 115B(9) inserted by Social Security Fraud Act 2001 (c. 11), s. 15(1).

CONSERVATION.
Stat. Def., "in relation to a living organism or type of habitat, includes the restoration or enhancement of a population or habitat" (Countryside and Rights of Way Act 2000 (c. 37), s. 74(7)).

CONSTRUCTION PURPOSES.
"Use for construction purposes", Stat. Def., Finance Act 2001 (c. 9), s. 48(2).

CONTRIBUTION.
Stat. Def., in relation to political party, Companies Act 1985 (c. 6), Sched. 7, para. 4(3), inserted by Political Parties, Elections and Referendums Act 2000 (c. 41), s. 140.

CONTROL (OF A COMPANY).
Stat. Def., Finance Act 2000 (c. 17), Sched. 22, para. 118.

COST BENEFIT ANALYSIS.
Stat. Def., Financial Services and Markets Act 2000 (c. 8), s. 65(11).

COUNSEL.
See AID, ABET, COUNSEL OR PROCURE.

COUNTRY.
See OPEN COUNTRY.

COURT.
Stat. Defs., Powers of Criminal Courts (Sentencing) Act 2000 (c. 6), s. 163 (excluding court-martial); Criminal Justice and Court Services Act 2000 (c. 43), s. 61(8) (including court-martial and Standing Civilian Court); same Act, s. 69(7) (excluding court-martial and Courts-Martial Appeal Court).

CRAFT.
See PLEASURE CRAFT.

CREDIT.
Stat. Def., "includes any cash loan or other financial accommodation" (Trustee Act 2000 (c. 29), s. 3(5)).

CRIME OF VIOLENCE.
A jury was entitled to conclude that an act of buggery was not a 'crime of violence'. *R. (August) v. Criminal Injuries Compensation Appeals Panel* [2001] 2 W.L.R. 1452 C.A, [2001] 2 All E.R. 874 C.A.

CRIME AGAINST HUMANITY.
Stat. Def., article 7 of the Statute of the International Criminal Court, done at Rome on July 17, 1998, as applied by section 50(1) of the International Criminal Court Act 2001 (c. 17) and as set out in Schedule 8 to that Act.

CRIMINAL CAUSE OR MATTER.
An order under section 77 of the Criminal Justice Act 1988 restraining a person from removing or disposing of assets is essentially civil in character and is not a "criminal cause or matter" (for the purpose of section 18(1)(a) of the Supreme Court Act 1981 (jurisdiction of Court of Appeal)) despite the fact that it is granted in consequence of criminal proceedings. *Government of the United States of America v. Montgomery* [2001] 1 W.L.R. 196 H.L., [2001] 1 All E.R. 815 H.L.

See also CHARGED WITH A CRIMINAL OFFENCE, CIVIL PRO-
CEEDINGS and CRIMINAL PROCEEDINGS.

CRIMINAL INVESTIGATION.
Stat. Def., Race Relations Act 1976 (c. 74), s. 57(4B) inserted by Race
Relations (Amendment) Act 2000 (c. 34), s.5.

CRIMINAL PROCEEDINGS.
Criminal proceedings involve a formal accusation by the state or a private
prosecution that a defendant has committed a breach of the criminal law and
amount to proceedings which may culminate in his conviction and condem-
nation. An application by Customs and Excise Commissioners for access
orders under paragraph 11 of Schedule 11 to the Value Added Tax Act 1994
(c. 24) was not criminal proceedings, because no formal accusation was made
and no proceedings begun which could have led to conviction, although the
taxpayers were indeed suspected by the Commissioners of the commission
of offences. *Customs and Excise Commissioners v. City of London Magistrates' Court* [2000] 1 W.L.R. 2020 Q.B.D, [2000] 4 All E.R. 763 Q.B.D.
    Stat. Def., Regulation of Investigatory Powers Act 2000 (c. 23), s. 81(4).
    Stat. Def., including various military proceedings, Freedom of Infor-
mation Act 2000 (c. 36), s. 30(5).
    See also CIVIL PROCEEDINGS, CHARGED WITH A CRIMINAL
OFFENCE and CRIMINAL CAUSE OR MATTER.

CRIME.
See FINANCIAL CRIME.

CURFEW ORDER.
Stat. Def., Powers of Criminal Courts (Sentencing) Act 2000 (c. 6), s. 37.

CURTILAGE.
The curtilage of a building need not always be a particularly small area.
What a building's curtilage amounts to is a question of fact and degree.
*Skerritts of Nottingham Ltd v. Secretary of State for the Environment,
Transport and the Regions* [2000] 3 W.L.R. 511 C.A.

CUSTODIAL SENTENCE.
Stat. Def., Powers of Criminal Courts (Sentencing) Act 2000 (c. 6), s. 76.

CUSTODY.
In relation to children. The term custody in relation to children has become
outdated in domestic law as a result of the Children Act 1989 (c. 41). But it is
still of importance in international conventions. For recent cases on the
meaning of the expression in that context see: *Re B. (A Minor) (Abduction)*
[1994] 2 F.L.R. 249; *McKiver v. McKiver (O.H.)* 1995 S.L.T. 790; *Pirrie v.
Sawacki* 1997 S.C.L.R. 59; *S. v. H.* 1997 3 W.L.R. 1086.
    In context of imprisonment. Whether a particular situation amounts to

being in custody will depend on the context. So, for example, contrast *R. v. National Insurance Commissioner, ex p. Timmis* [1955] 1 Q.B. 139 (where detention in a mental institution was custody for the purposes of the National Insurance Act 1946 (c. 67)) with *R. v. Straffen* [1952] 2 Q.B. 911 (where detention in Broadmoor was not custody within the meaning of the Judges' Rules as to the administering of cautions). Note also (a) that a child convicted by a juvenile court and committed to the care of the local authority was not in custody for the purpose of the Courts Act 1971 (c. 23), s. 13(4)(b) (*R. v. K.* [1978] 1 W.L.R. 139) and (b) that a conditional discharge did <u>not</u> amount to a non-custodial sentence for the purpose of the Criminal Justice Act 1982 (c. 48), s. 1(4A) (*R. v. Hunter* [1991] Crim. L.R. 146 and *R. v. Betts (Mark)* (1992) 13 Cr. App. R. (S.) 281).

In other contexts. Holding a dog's lead while under its owner's supervision does not amount to being in custody of the dog — *Royal Society for the Prevention of Cruelty to Animals v. Miller* March 8, 1994 T.L.R.

For "custody or control" of documents see *London & Yorkshire Bank v. Cooper* 15 Q.B.D. 7 and the unreported case of *Roake, West and Smith v. Butler* noted in [1963] C.L. 3066.

CYCLE TRACK.
Stat. Def., Countryside and Rights of Way Act 2000 (c. 37), s. 60(5).

DEBT.
See SIMPLE CONTRACT DEBT.

DECISION.
The passing of sensitive personal information between one public authority and another did not amount to a "decision" attracting an obligation that required to be judged according to the principles of procedural fairness. *R. (A) v. Chief Constable of C.* [2001] 1 W.L.R. 461 Q.B.D.

DECOMMISSIONING (OF PLANT OR MACHINERY).
Stat. Def., Capital Allowances Act 2001 (c. 2), s. 163(4A) inserted by Finance Act 2001 (c. 9), Sched. 20, para. 6.

DEGRADING.
See INHUMAN.

DELIVERY.
Where the seller of goods who is in possession of them acknowledges that he holds them on the buyer's account and that the buyer is entitled to possess them as owner and that the seller is a mere bailee with possession, the transaction amounts to delivery to the buyer followed by redelivery to the seller as bailee. *Michael Gerson (Leasing) Ltd v. Wilkinson* [2001] 1 All E.R. 148 C.A.

DEMERGER (OF COMPANY).
Stat. Def., Finance Act 2000 (c. 17), Sched. 22, para. 121(1).

DEMOLITION.
"Partial demolition" distinguished from alteration: see PARTIAL DEMOLITION.

DEVELOPMENT.
See RESEARCH AND DEVELOPMENT.

DEVOLUTION ISSUE.
Within the meaning of Scotland Act 1998 (c. 46), Sched. 6, para. 1(b) — see *Hoekstra v. H.M. Advocate* [2000] 3 W.L.R. 1817 P.C.

DIRECTOR.
"Shadow director". The expression was given a loose and purposive construction so as to refer to anyone other than a professional adviser who

had real influence in the corporate affairs of a company, whether or not over all of its activities. *Secretary of State for Trade v. Deverell* [2000] 2 W.L.R. 907 C.A.

In relation to body corporate, Stat. Defs., Financial Services and Markets Act 2000 (c. 8), s. 417(1); Private Security Industry Act 2001 (c. 12), s. 25(1).

DISABLED.
The statutory definition of "disabled" in section 17(11) of the Children Act 1989 was expressly approved and applied for a different purpose by Hale L.J. in *Parkinson v. St. James Hospital* [2001] 3 All E.R. 97 C.A.

DISABLED PERSON.
Stat. Defs., Care Standards Act 2000 (c. 14), s. 121(2); Transport Act 2000 (c. 38), s. 146.

DISABLED PERSON'S BADGE.
Stat. Def., Terrorism Act 2000 (c. 11), s. 52.

DISMISSAL.
The reference to dismissal in section 4(2)(c) of the Race Relations Act 1976 — which makes it unlawful for an employer to discriminate against an employee on racial grounds by 'dismissing' him or her — includes constructive dismissal. *Derby Specialist Fabrication Ltd v. Burton* [2001] 2 All E.R. 840 E.A.T.

DISORDER (IN CONTEXT OF PUBLIC ORDER).
Stat. Def., Football Spectators Act 1989 (c. 37), s. 14C(2) inserted by Football (Disorder) Act 2000 (c. 25), Sched. 1, para. 2.

DISPOSAL.
For the purposes of section 128(2) of the Local Government Act 1972 — which protected the validity of a disposal of land despite lack of a required Ministerial consent — a disposal occurred on conveyance not on entry into a contract for sale. *Structadene Ltd v. Hackney London Borough Council* [2001] 2 All E.R. 225 Q.B.D.

Stat. Def., "includes the granting of an interest in or right over" property (Health and Social Care Act 2001 (c. 15), Sched. 1, para. 19).

DISPOSITION.
A payment made by a company to a creditor by a cheque drawn on a bank account in credit was a disposition of property in favour of the creditor but not a disposition in favour of the bank, which was a mere agent. *Hollicourt (Contracts) Ltd v. Bank of Ireland* [2001] 2 W.L.R. 290 C.A.

DOCUMENT.
Stat. Defs., Electronic Communications Act 2000 (c. 7), s. 15(1) ("includes a map, plan, design, drawing, picture or other image"); Financial Services and

Markets Act 2000 (c. 8), s. 417(1) ("includes information recorded in any form and, in relation to information recorded otherwise than in legible form, references to its production include references to producing a copy of the information in legible form").

See ADVERTISEMENT: "Advertisement or other document".

DOMESTIC BURGLARY.
Stat. Def., Powers of Criminal Courts (Sentencing) Act 2000 (c. 6), s. 111(5) ("a burglary committed in respect of a building or part of a building which is a dwelling").

DONATION.
Stat. Def., in context of political party, Political Parties, Elections and Referendums Act 2000 (c. 41), s. 50.

DRIVER.
For construction of the highly specialised definition of "driver" in Council Regulation 3820/85 [1985] O.J. L370/1 (on the harmonisation of certain social legislation relating to road transport) see *Vehicle Inspectorate v. Southern Coaches Limited* [2000] 2 C.M.L.R. 887 Q.B.D.

DWELLING.
Stat. Def., Representation of the People Act 1983 (c. 2) Act 2000 (c.), s. 202(1) as amended by Representation of the People Act 2000 (c. 2), Sched. 1, para. 22(a) ("includes any part of a building where that part is occupied separately as a dwelling"); Stat. Def., Terrorism Act 2000 (c. 11), s. 121 ("means a building or part of a building used as a dwelling, and a vehicle which is habitually stationary and which is used as a dwelling").

DWELLING-HOUSE.
A houseboat is not a dwelling-house for the purposes of section 1(1) of the Housing Act 1988 (c. 50) ("tenancy under which a dwelling-house is let") even where the agreement for the hiring of the boat is constructed along the same lines as a residential lease. *Chelsea Yacht and Boat Co. Ltd v. Pope* [2000] 1 W.L.R. 1941 C.A., [2001] 2 All E.R. 409 CA.

E

ECONOMIC LOSS.
The expression "economic loss" in section 21 of the Electricity Act 1989 (c. 29) did not mean the same as "pure economic loss" as it is used in the context of tort. So held the Court of Appeal — relying on statements of Ministers recorded in Hansard under the rule in *Pepper v. Hart* [1993] A.C. 593 — in *A. E. Beckett & Sons v. Midland Electricity p.l.c.* [2001] 1 W.L.R. 291 C.A.

EDITION.
The frame of reference for the term "published edition" is the language of the publishing trade and an "edition" is the product which the publisher offers to the public. *Newspaper Licensing Agency Ltd v. Marks & Spencer plc* [2001] 3 W.L.R. 290 H.L., [2001] 3 All E.R. 977 H.L.

EIUSDEM GENERIS.
See OTHER.

EJUSDEM GENERIS.
See OTHER.

ELECTRONIC COMMUNICATION.
Stat. Def., Electronic Communications Act 2000 (c. 7), s. 15(1).

ELECTRONIC SIGNATURE.
Stat. Def., Electronic Communications Act 2000 (c. 7), s. 7(2) ("an electronic signature is so much of anything in electronic form as — (a) is incorporated into or otherwise logically associated with any electronic communication or electronic data; and (b) purports to be so incorporated or associated for the purpose being used in establishing the authenticity of the communication or data, the integrity of the communication or data, or both"); for a similar but not identical definition see Regulation of Investigatory Powers Act 2000 (c. 23), s. 56(1).

EMOLUMENTS.
Payments to employees on the determination of employment made in accordance with a contractual term agreed at the commencement of

employment are emoluments for the purposes of Case I of Schedule D in section 19(1) of the Income and Corporation Taxes Act 1988. *E.M.I. Group Electronics Ltd v. Coldicott (Inspector of Taxes)* [2000] 1 W.L.R. 540 C.A.

EMPLOYEE.
For a discussion of the status of agency workers in relation to employment, see N.L.J. September 14, 2001, pp. 1310–11.

Stat. Def., "means a person employed under a contract of service or apprenticeship, whether express or implied, and (if express) whether oral or in writing" (Transport Act 2000 (c. 38), s. 182(4)).

ENACTMENT.
A Council Regulation is an enactment for the purpose of section 170(2) of the Customs and Excise Management Act 1979 (fraudulent evasion of prohibition or restriction in respect of goods under an enactment). *R. v. Sissen* [2001] 1 W.L.R. 902 C.A.

Stat. Def., including provision of Measure of the Church Assembly or of the General Synod of the Church of England, Trustee Act 2000 (c. 29), s. 39(1).

ENCLOSED AREA.
Section 4 of the Vagrancy Act 1824 provides that "every person being found in or upon any dwelling-house, warehouse coach-house, stable or outhouse, or in any enclosed yard, garden or area, for any unlawful purpose ... shall be deemed a rogue and vagabond ...". The Divisional Court held that a true construction of the expression "enclosed area" in this context excludes a room within a building: the context implies an area in the open air. *Talbot v. Director of Public Prosecutions* [2000] 1 W.L.R. 1102 Q.B.D.

EQUIPMENT.
Stat. Def., "includes vehicles, apparatus, furniture, fittings, accoutrements and clothing" (Police (Northern Ireland) Act 2000 (c. 32), s. 77(1)).

ESSOIN.
Essoin is an excuse from attending on a summons to court (Glanvill I, 8–33).

ESTATE.
In the context of the School Sites Act 1841, which provides for reverter of land to the estate of the original grantor upon a change of use, "estate" referred not to a specific physical area of land but to the precise legal concept of the common law scheme for the temporal division of land holdings into interests of different duration. *Fraser v. Canterbury Diocesan Board of Finance* [2001] 2 W.L.R. 1103 C.A.

EVIDENCE.
"Sufficient evidence". Note that "sufficient evidence" has a technical meaning in Scots law, namely a kind of evidence that does not require to be

corroborated. So an enactment which applies both to England and Wales and to Scotland uses "where sufficient evidence is adduced to raise an issue ..." only in those parts which cannot affect Scotland, and otherwise uses the longer form "where evidence is adduced which is sufficient to raise an issue ...". See Terrorism Act 2000 (c. 11), s. 118, and explanation given by Lord Bassam of Brighton (Parliamentary Under-Secretary of State, Home Office) in moving an amendment on Lords Report.

EXCEPTIONAL.
A helpful general observation about the construction of "exceptional" is found in the context of section 2 of the Crime (Sentences) Act 1997 (exceptional circumstances which justify not imposing a sentence of life imprisonment). Lord Bingham of Cornhill C.J. said in his judgment in *R.v. Kelly (Edward)* [2000] Q.B. 198, 208: "We must construe 'exceptional' as an ordinary, familiar English adjective, and not as a term of art. It describes a circumstance which is such as to form an exception, which is out of the ordinary course, or unusual, or special, or uncommon. To be exceptional a circumstance need not be unique, or unprecedented, or very rare; but it cannot be one that is regularly, or routinely, or normally encountered.". Cited by Lord Woolf C.J. in *R. v. Offen* [2001] 1 W.L.R. 253, 269.

EXPERT.
Stat. Def., Financial Services and Markets Act 2000 (c. 8), Sched. 10, para. 8 ("includes any engineer, valuer, accountant or other person whose profession, qualifications or experience give authority to a statement made by him").

EXPLOSIVE.
Stat. Def., Terrorism Act 2000 (c. 11), s. 121.

F

FALSE INSTRUMENT.
An instrument is false for the purposes of section 9(1)(g) of the Forgery and Counterfeiting Act 1981 if it is a document which required, before it could be made or altered, that there should exist or should have existed a set of circumstances and those circumstances did not exist or had not existed a set of circumstances and those circumstances did not exist or had not existed. So a tachograph record sheet could be a false instrument. *Attorney-General's Reference (No. 1 of 2000)* [2001] 1 W.L.R. 331 C.A.

FAMILY.
The House of Lords decided, reversing the Court of Appeal, that a homosexual partner is not included in a reference to a spouse but can be included in a reference to a person's family. *Fitzpatrick v. Sterling Housing Association Ltd* [1993] 3 W.L.R. 1113 H.L. For comment on the case see [2000] Cambridge Law Journal vol. 59, Part I, pp. 39–42.

FEMALE.
A person was a female at the time of (and for the purposes of validating) her marriage to another person where at that time —
  (1) her genetic and gonadal sex was male, but
  (2) her genitalia were ambiguous, and
  (3) her body habitus and gender orientation appeared to be female, and
  (4) she had chosen to live as a woman before having hormone treatment and gender reassignment surgery, and
  (5) although before surgery she would have been unable to have sexual intercourse at all, after surgery she was capable of consummating the marriage as a woman. (*W. v. W. (Physical Inter-sex)* [2001] 2 W.L.R. 674 Fam. D.)

FETA.
The European Court of Justice had to consider whether Feta has become a generic description of a kind of cheese or whether it designates a product as being of Greek origin or as being manufactured using sheep's or goat's milk — *Denmark v. E.C. Commission* [2001] 1 C.M.L.R. 14 E.C.J. The judgment is not conclusive on the point: Commission Regulation 1107/96 was annulled to the extent to which it registered Feta as a protected designation of origin, but only because the Court held that the Commission had ignored relevant

matters in reaching its conclusion on the point. The Commission may, presumably, therefore treat the matter as remitted to it and reach the same conclusion based on the wider class of considerations.

FINAL SETTLEMENT.
See FULL AND FINAL SETTLEMENT.

FINANCIAL ACTIVITIES.
Stat. Def., Finance Act 2000 (c. 17), Sched. 15, para. 11(2).

FINANCIAL CRIME.
Stat. Def., Financial Services and Markets Act 2000 (c. 8), s. 6(3) ("includes any offence involving — (a) fraud or dishonesty; (b) misconduct in, or misuse of information relating to, a financial market; or (c) handling the proceeds of crime").

FINE.
In judicial context, Stat. Def., Powers of Criminal Courts (Sentencing) Act 2000 (c. 6), s. 78(5).

FINGERPRINT.
Stat. Def., Police and Criminal Justice Act 1984 (c. 60), s. 65(1) substituted by Criminal Justice and Police Act 2001 (c. 16), s. 78(8).

FIREARM.
Stat. Def. (including air gun and air pistol), Terrorism Act 2000 (c. 11), s. 121.

FIRM.
Stat. Def., Financial Services and Markets Act 2000 (c. 8), s. 31(4) ("means a partnership or an unincorporated association of persons").

FISH.
Stat. Def., including shellfish, Capital Allowances Act 2001 (c. 2), s. 41(5).

FISH FARMING.
Stat. Def., "the intensive rearing, on a commercial basis, of fish intended for human consumption" (Capital Allowances Act 2001 (c. 2), s. 41(5)).

FISHING.
Stat. Def., Capital Allowances Act 2001 (c. 2), s. 41(5).

FIXED.
The critical feature which distinguishes a "fixed" charge from a "floating" charge is the chargor's ability, freely and without the chargee's consent, to control and manage the charged assets and withdraw them from the security. *Agnew v. Commissioner of Inland Revenue* [2001] 3 W.L.R. 454 P.C.

FIXTURE.
Stat. Def., "means machinery or plant that is so installed or otherwise fixed in or to a building or other description of land as to become, in law, part of that building or other land" and "includes any boiler, or water-filled radiator, installed in a building as part of a space or water heating system" (Capital Allowances Act 2001 (c. 2), s. 173.

FLAT (IN CONTEXT OF DWELLING).
Stat. Def., Capital Allowances Act 2001 (c. 2), s. 393A(3) inserted by Finance Act 2001 (c. 9), Sched. 19.

FLOATING.
"Floating charge" differentiated from "fixed charge" — see FIXED.

FOR THE MOST PART.
For the purpose of Annex I to Council Directive 93/37/EEC on public works contracts a body is financed for the most part by the state or other public bodies if taking all of the body's sources of income into account for a particular year more than half of the total came from public sources. *R. v. Her Majesty's Treasury, ex p. University of Cambridge* (Case C-380/98) [2000] 1 W.L.R. 2514 E.C.J.

FORECAST.
Stat. Def., Representation of the People Act 1983 (c. 2), s. 66A(4) inserted by Representation of the People Act 2000 (c. 2), Sched. 6, para. 6 ("includes estimate").

FORESTRY.
Stat. Def., Finance Act 2001 (c. 9), s. 48(1).

FORGERY.
See FALSE INSTRUMENT.

FOSTERING AGENCY.
Stat. Def., Care Standards Act 2000 (c. 14), s. 4(4).

FRAUD.
For the purposes of section 281(3) of the Insolvency Act 1986 (which prevents release from bankruptcy debts incurred in respect of "fraud" or "fraudulent breach of trust") the expression "fraud" means actual fraud and does not include constructive fraud such as undue influence. Constructive

fraud includes a range of matters some of which do not involve actual dishonesty. If Parliament had intended to preserve liability for the full range of these matters, some wide language would have been used. *Mander v. Evans* [2001] 3 All E.R. 811 Ch.

FROM.
In reckoning periods of time a reference to a period "from" a day normally has the effect of excluding that day from the reckoning. *Zoan v. Rouamba* [2000] 1 W.L.R. 1509 C.A.

FULL AND FINAL SETTLEMENT.
Where a plaintiff has overlapping claims for successive breaches of contract against two defendants and concludes an agreement expressed to be "in final settlement" with one defendant, the words used have to be interpreted in the circumstances to determine whether the intention was to have any effect, and if so what, on the plaintiff's claim against the other defendant. *Heaton v. AXA Equity & Law Life Assurance Society P.L.C.* [2000] 3 W.L.R. 1341 C.A, [2000] 4 All E.R. 673 C.A.

An agreement signed by employees made compulsorily redundant by a bank and expressed to be "in full and final settlement of all or any claims ... of whatsoever nature that exist or may exist" against the bank was not sufficient to release the bank from liability in matters that could not have been in the contemplation of either party at the time. *Bank of Credit and Commerce International SA v. Ali* [2001] 2 W.L.R. 735 H.L., [2001] 1 All E.R. 961 H.L.

FUR FARM.
For a — non-express — definition of a fur farm see Fur Farming (Prohibition) Act 2000 (c. 33), s.1.

G

GENOCIDE.
Stat. Def., article 6 of the Statute of the International Criminal Court, done at Rome on July 17, 1998, as applied by section 50(1) of the International Criminal Court Act 2001 (c. 17) and as set out in Schedule 8 to that Act.

GOODS.
Fishing rights did not constitute "goods" for the purposes of Community law relating to the free movement of goods. *Peter Jagerskiold v. Torolf Gustafsson* (Case C-97/98) [2000] 1 C.M.L.R. 235 E.C.J.

GOODS VEHICLE.
Stat. Def., Income and Corporation Taxes Act 1988 (c. 1), Sched. 12AA, para. 3(6) inserted by Finance Act 2001 (c. 9), Sched. 12.

GOVERNMENT DEPARTMENT.
Stat. Defs., Regulation of Investigatory Powers Act 2000 (c. 23), s. 4(8) ("includes any part of the Scottish Administration, a Northern Ireland department and the National Assembly for Wales"); Postal Services Act 2000 (c. 26), s. 7(5) ("includes any Minister of the Crown, any part of the Scottish Administration, the National Assembly for Wales, the Northern Ireland Assembly, any Northern Ireland Minister or Northern Ireland junior Minister and any Northern Ireland department"); Freedom of Information Act 2000 (c. 36), s. 84 (including, in particular and subject to express exception, "any other body or authority exercising statutory functions on behalf of the Crown").

GRAPHIC.
Drawings could be "graphic work" for the purposes of section 4(1)(a) of the Copyright, Design and Patents Act 1988 despite the fact that they were not exclusively pictorial but needed, in order to be understood, figures and words which appeared on them. *Vermaat v. Boncrest Limited, The Times,* June 23, 2000 Ch. (Distinguishing *Interlego A.G., v. Tyco Industries Inc* [1989] A.C. 217).

GRAVEL.
Stat. Def., Finance Act 2001 (c. 9), s. 48(1).

H

HEATING APPLIANCE.
Stat. Def., Value Added Tax Act 1994 (c. 23), Sched. 7A, Note 4, inserted by Finance Act 2001 (c. 9), Sched. 31(1).

HER.
See THEIR.

HIS.
See THEIR.

HOSPITAL.
Stat. Def., Care Standards Act 2000 (c. 14), s. 2(3).

HOUSEBOAT.
For discussion of the nature of a houseboat with reference to a number of decided cases see New Law Journal, March 23, 2001 pages 419–20 and [2001] Cambridge Law Journal 40–43.

HUSBANDRY.
Stat. Def., Capital Allowances Act 2001 (c. 2), s. 362.

IMPRISONMENT.
See SENTENCE OF IMPRISONMENT.

IN ACCORDANCE WITH THE LAW.
The expression "in accordance with the law" in Article 8 of the European Convention on Human Rights (which prohibits interference with certain rights unless they are in accordance with the law) implies conditions which go beyond the existence of a legal basis in domestic law and requires that the legal basis be accessible and foreseeable. *Foxley v. United Kingdom* (Application No. 33274/96) 8 Butterworths Human Rights Cases 571 European Court of Human Rights, June 20, 2000.

IN PARTICULAR.
A statutory instrument (the Housing Benefit (General) Regulations 1987, reg. 11(2)) which required a local authority to reduce a person's rent by such amount as it considered appropriate "having regard in particular to the cost of suitable alternative accommodation elsewhere" did not exclude consideration of factors other than the one particularised. *R. v. City of Westminster Housing Benefit Review Board, ex p. Mehanne* [2001] 2 All E.R. 690 H.L. ([2001] U.K.H.L./11).

IN REMUNERATIVE WORK.
See WORK.

IN WORK.
See WORK.

IN WRITING.
See WRITING.

INFORMATION.
Stat. Def., Private Security Industry Act 2001 (c. 12), s. 25(1).

INHUMAN.
For the notion that treatment is not "inhuman or degrading" where it is administered for necessary therapeutic purposes, see the cases discussed

towards the end of Dame Elizabeth Butler-Sloss P's judgment in *N.H.S. Trust A. v. M.* [2001] 2 W.L.R. 942 Fam.

[INHUMAN.]
This word has become of particular importance in the context of the phrase "inhuman or degrading treatment or punishment" since the passing of the Human Rights Act 1998 (c. 42) and the consequent adoption of Article 3 of the European Convention on Human Rights. *Stroud* is not the place for an exhaustive treatise on the interpretation of this phrase which is at the heart of a very large number of cases before international and domestic forums every year. But it is possible to indicate cases and resources of particular significance on the meaning of the phrase. A helpful article on the meaning of the phrase in relation to prisoners, will be found in N.L.J. August 10, 2001 at pp. 1222 & 26.

INNER LONDON.
Stat. Def., Countryside and Rights of Way Act 2000 (c. 37), s. 45(1).

INSURANCE TRANSACTION.
A co-operative arrangement under which one insurance company ran the business of another in return for remuneration at market rates, but without assuming the related liabilities, and under which the other company concluded insurance contracts in its own name, did not constitute an insurance transaction within the meaning of article 13(B)(a) of the Sixth Directive 77/388 on the harmonisation of turnover taxes. *Re Forsakringsaktiebolaget Skandia (Publ) (Case C–240/99)* [2001] 2 C.M.L.R. 34 E.C.J., [2001] 1 W.L.R. 1617 E.C.J.

INTELLECTUAL PROPERTY.
Stat. Def., "means (a) any patent, trade mark, registered design, copyright, design right, performer's right or plant breeder's right; and (b) any rights under the law of a country or territory outside the United Kingdom which correspond or are similar to those falling within paragraph (a)" (Finance Act 2000 (c. 17), Sched. 14, para. 24(6)); see also different definition in Sched. 20, para. 7.

INTERCEPT.
In context of intercepting a communication, Stat. Def., Regulation of Investigatory Powers Act 2000 (c. 23), s. 2(2) to (5).

INTEREST.
For "material interest" in a company, see MATERIAL INTEREST.

INTEREST (IN LAND).
Stat. Def., of an extensive kind, Capital Allowances Act 2001 (c. 2), s. 175.

INTERNATIONAL COURT.
Stat. Def., Freedom of Information Act 2000 (c. 36), s. 27(5).

INVESTIGATION.
Section 7 of the Road Traffic Act 1988 permits a constable to require the provision of a specimen "in the course of an investigation into whether a person has committed an offence" under specified provisions. In this context "investigation" is not to be construed "as requiring any such greater formality than the ordinary plain meaning of the word would normally involve": May L.J. in *Graham v. Albert* [1985] R.T.R. 352.
   See also IN THE COURSE OF.

INVESTMENT.
Stat. Def., Financial Services and Markets Act 2000 (c. 8), s. 21(14) ("includes any asset, right or interest").

J

JUDICIAL AUTHORITY.
Stat. Def., Regulation of Investigatory Powers Act 2000 (c. 23), s. 65(11).

JUDICIAL REVIEW.
Judicial Review proceedings are not "brought by or at the instigation of a public authority" — the Crown's involvement is purely nominal — *R (Ben-Abdelaziz and another) v. Haringey London Borough Council* [2001] 1 W.L.R. 1485 C.A.

K

KEEPER.
There could be more than one "keeper" of a horse at a time for the purposes of the Animals Act 1971 (having regard to the definition in section 6(3)). *Flack v. Hudson* [2001] 2 W.L.R. 982 CA.

KEY (IN RELATION TO ELECTRONIC DATA).
Stat. Def., Regulation of Investigatory Powers Act 2000 (c. 23), s. 56(1).

KNEW.
The Second EEC Motor Insurance Directive 84/5/EEC of December 30, 1983 allows member states to exclude compensation for injuries caused by uninsured vehicles in cases where the injured person voluntarily entered a vehicle and "knew that it was uninsured" (Article 1(4). The House of Lords held that in this context "knew" included "a category of case which is so close to actual knowledge that the law generally treats a person as having knowledge": the type of case where "a passenger had information from which he drew the conclusion that the driver might well not be insured but deliberately refrained from asking questions lest his suspicions should be confirmed. He wanted not to know". The court decided that "knew" in this context was therefore coextensive with the phrase "knew or ought to have known" in the Motor Insurers' Bureau 1988 agreement with the Government. *White v. White* [2001] 1 W.L.R. 481 H.L., [2001] 2 All E.R. 43 H.L.

KNEW OR OUGHT TO HAVE KNOWN.
See KNEW.

KNOWINGLY.
For the purpose of the offence of being knowingly concerned in the fraudulent evasion of a prohibition on the importation of goods it is sufficient for the prosecutor to prove that the defendant knew that the operation on which he was engaged involved prohibited goods and was designed to evade a prohibition on their importation. It is not necessary to prove that the defendant knew the nature of the goods in question. *R. v. Forbes (Giles)* [2001] 3 W.L.R. 428 H.L., [2001] 4 All E.R. 97 H.L.

KNOWLEDGE.
See BLIND EYE KNOWLEDGE.
　See also KNEW.

L

LAW.
See POINT OF LAW.
   See also IN ACCORDANCE WITH THE LAW.

LAW OFFICERS.
See THE LAW OFFICERS.

LEARNING DISABILITY.
Stat. Def., "a state of arrested or incomplete development of mind which includes significant impairment of intelligence and social functioning" (Disabled Persons (Services, Consultation and Representation Act 1986 (c. 33), s. 11(2) substituted by Health and Social Care Act 2001 (c. 15), s. 62(3)).

LEASE.
Stat. Defs., Income and Corporation Taxes Act 1988 (c. 1), s. 43G(2) inserted by Finance Act 2000 (c. 17), s. 110 ("includes an underlease, sublease, tenancy or licence and an agreement for any of those things, but does not include a mortgage or heritable security"); Capital Allowances Act 2001 (c. 2), s. 70(6) (similar definition).

LEASING.
Stat. Def., Capital Allowances Act 2001 (c. 2), s. 105.

LEFT.
An insurance policy did not cover the insured for theft of a car where the keys "have been left in or on the car". The Court of Appeal held that the quoted words were not to be given any technical or special meaning and that the keys had been "left" in the car even where the insured was just a few yards away paying for petrol at a garage. *Hayward v. Union Insurance* New Law Journal May 18, 2001 pp. 718–19.

LETTER.
Stat. Def., Postal Services Act 2000 (c. 26), s. 125(1).

LIMESTONE.
Stat. Def., Finance Act 2001 (c. 9), s. 48(1).

LIMITED LIABILITY PARTNERSHIP.
This is a statutory creation, see the Limited Liability Partnerships Act 2000 (c. 12).

LIVESTOCK.
Stat. Def., Countryside and Rights of Way Act 2000 (c. 37), s. 45(1).

LOCAL AUTHORITY.
Stat. Def., Local Government Act 2000 (c. 22), s. 1.

LOCAL GOVERNMENT.
For a list of bodies with local government functions see the Race Relations (Amendment) Act 2000 (c. 34), Sched. 1 paras 12 to 45.

LOCK (AS NOUN).
Stat. Def., Private Security Industry Act 2001 (c. 12), Sched. 2, para. 6(4).

LONDON.
See INNER LONDON.

LOSS.
See ECONOMIC LOSS.

M

MAER.
An alternative style for a person who is an elected mayor of a local authority in Wales: Stat. Def., Local Government Act 2000 (c. 22), s. 39(3).

MAIL-BAG.
Stat. Def., Postal Services Act 2000 (c. 26), s. 125(1).

MAINTAIN.
For the construction of a local authority's statutory duty to maintain a highway see *Goodes v. East Sussex County Council* [2000] 1 W.L.R. 1356 H.L., [2000] 3 All E.R. 603 H.L.

MALE.
See FEMALE.

MARKET VALUE.
Stat. Defs., "in relation to any property, means the price which might reasonably be expected to be paid for the property on a sale in the open market" (Political Parties, Elections and Referendums Act 2000 (c. 41), s. 160(1)); "in relation to any asset, means the price the asset would fetch in the open market" (Capital Allowances Act 2001 (c. 2), s. 577(1)).

MATERIAL INTEREST (IN A COMPANY).
Stat. Def., Finance Act 2000 (c. 17), Sched. 14, para. 31.

MAY.
A provision that a blood sample "may" be taken from a child with his parent's consent meant that a sample could not be taken without consent. *Re O (a child) (blood tests: constraint)* [2000] 2 All E.R. 29 Fam. D., construing Family Law Reform Act 1969 (c. 46), s. 21(3).

MAYOR.
The style to which a person is entitled as the elected mayor of a local authority in England or in Wales: Stat. Def., Local Government Act 2000 (c. 22), s. 39(2) & (3).

MEETING.
See PUBLIC MEETING.

MEETING ROOM.
Stat. Def., "means any room which it is the practice to let for public meetings" (Political Parties, Elections and Referendums Act 2000 (c. 41), Sched. 12, para. 2(6).

MENTAL DISORDER.
Stat. Def., Care Standards Act 2000 (c. 14), s. 121(1).

MERGER (OF COMPANY).
Stat. Def., Finance Act 2000 (c. 17), Sched. 22, para. 121.

MILITARY OFFICER.
Stat. Def., Army Act 1955 (c. 18), s. 83ZC(4) inserted by Armed Forces Discipline Act 2000 (c. 4), s. 16(1) ("an officer belonging to Her Majesty's military forces and subject to military law").

MINERAL ASSET.
Stat. Def., Capital Allowances Act 2001 (c. 2), s. 397.

MINIBUS.
Stat. Def., "a vehicle constructed or adapted for the carriage of passengers which has a seating capacity of 9 or more, but less than 12" (Income and Corporation Taxes Act 1988 (c. 1), s. 197AA(3) inserted by Finance Act 2001 (c. 9), s. 60(4) (and see also section 197AA(9) inserted by same section for determination of seating capacity)).

MINISTERIAL COMMUNICATIONS.
Stat. Def., Freedom of Information Act 2000 (c. 36), s. 35(5).

MINISTERIAL PRIVATE OFFICE.
Stat. Def., Freedom of Information Act 2000 (c. 36), s. 35(5).

MISCONDUCT.
See WILFUL MISCONDUCT.

MISFEASANCE IN PUBLIC OFFICE.
The nature of this tort is discussed extensively in *Three Rivers District Council v. Bank of England* [2001] 2 All E.R. 513 H.L. ([2001] U.K.H.L./16).

MISREPRESENTATION.
The unreported case of *Ward v. Stevens* referred to in the last paragraph under this entry in the main work was decided on October 7, 1992 in the Norwich County Court.

MIXED.
Stat. Def., "includes blended", Finance Act 2001 (c. 9), s. 48(1).

MODIFICATIONS.
Stat. Def., Representation of the People Act 2000 (c. 2), s. 17(2) ("includes additions, omissions and amendments (and 'modify' has a corresponding meaning").

MOTOR SALVAGE OPERATOR.
Stat. Def., Vehicles (Crime) Act 2001 (c. 3), s. 1.

MOTOR SALVAGE YARD.
Stat. Def., Vehicles (Crime) Act 2001 (c. 3), s. 16(1).

MOTOR CAR.
See CAR.

MOTOR VEHICLE.
Stat. Def., "any vehicle whose function is or was to be used on roads as a mechanically propelled vehicle" (Scrap Metal Dealers Act 1964 (c. 69), s. 4A(7) inserted by Vehicles (Crime) Act 2001 (c. 3), s. 35).

MOUNTAIN.
Stat. Def., Countryside and Rights of Way Act 2000 (c. 37), s. 1(2).

MUST HAVE PARTICULAR REGARD.
"It was submitted that the phrase 'must have particular regard to' indicates that the court should place extra weight on the matters to which the subsection refers. I do not so read it. Rather it points to the need for the court to consider the matters to which the subsection refers specifically and separately from other relevant considerations. On the facts of this case I do not think that it makes any difference how the phrase is interpreted".: Sir Andrew Morritt V.-C. in *Ashdown v. Telegraph Group* [2001] 2 All E.R. 370, 383 Ch.

NATIONAL SECURITY.
The security of the United Kingdom is increasingly dependant on the security of other countries and the government is therefore entitled to treat the promotion of terrorism against any State by a person in the United Kingdom as a threat to national security. *Home Secretary v. Rehman* [2000] 3 W.L.R. 1240 C.A.

NATIONALITY.
For the purposes of Community law the question of whether a person has United Kingdom nationality is determined by the United Kingdom's 1982 Declaration replacing the 1972 Declaration which was annexed to the Treaty on the United Kingdom's accession. The effectiveness and legality of the Declarations were challenged unsuccessfully in *R. v. Secretary of State for the Home Department, ex parte Manjit Kaur* [2001] 2 C.M.L.R. 24 E.C.J.

NECESSARY.
For a general discussion of how "necessary" is construed in various contexts by the European Court of Justice and others (particularly in the context of balancing rights of one person with necessary interests of the public, and so on) see *Ashworth v. MGN* [2001] 1 All E.R. 991 CA, especially *per* Lord Phillips M.R. at pp. 1009–11.

NECESSARY DISBURSEMENT.
The payment by liquidator of corporation tax on post-liquidation profits was a "necessary disbursement" within the meaning of rule 4.218(1)(m) of the Insolvency Rules 1986 (No. 1925). *In re Toshoku Finance U.K. P.L.C.* [2000] 1 W.L.R. 2478 C.A.

NEIGHBOUR.
In Schedule 2 of the Housing Act 1985 (c. 68) the expression "neighbours" was not confined to adjoining occupiers but included people living sufficiently close to the behaviour creating a nuisance or annoyance to be adversely affected by it. *Northampton Borough Council v. Lovatt* (The Independent, November 14, 1997).

NUCLEAR WEAPON.
Stat. Def., Terrorism Act 2000 (c. 11), s. 55.

NURSES AGENCY.
Stat. Def., Care Standards Act 2000 (c. 14), s. 4(5).

NURSING HOME.
Stat. Def., Finance Act 2000 (c. 17), Sched. 14, para. 25(2).

OFFENCE.
See SEXUAL OFFENCE and VIOLENT OFFENCE.

OFFENSIVE WEAPON.
Stat. Def., Armed Forces Act 2001 (c. 19), s. 2(10).

OFFICER.
See MILITARY OFFICER.
   Of body corporate, Stat. Def., Television Licences (Disclosure of Information) Act 2000 (c. 15), s. 4(3).

OPEN COUNTRY.
Stat. Def., Countryside and Rights of Way Act 2000 (c. 37), s. 1(2).

OPTION.
Stat. Def., "means any right to acquire shares" (Finance Act 2000 (c. 17), Sched. 14, para. 71(1).

ORDINARY SHARE CAPITAL.
Stat. Def., Finance Act 2000 (c. 17), Sched. 15, para. 7(2).

ORGANISATION.
The phrase "clubs, societies or other organisations" did not include a local authority, by application of the eiusdem generis rule. So held Neuberger J. in *Phonographic Performance Ltd v. South Tyneside MBC* [2001] W.L.R. 400 Ch. in a judgment citing a very helpful exposition of the eiusdem generis rule by Lord Diplock in *Quazi v. Quazi* [1980] A.C. 744, 807–8 (for which see OTHER).
   Stat. Def. (including any association or combination of persons), Terrorism Act 2000 (c. 11), s. 121.

OTHER.
Where a statute uses the expression "and other [whatever]", the potential breadth of whatever word falls within the square brackets when taken out of context will be restricted by reference to what went before.
   This is the most common application of the *eiusdem generis* rule, which is helpfully expounded by Lord Diplock in *Quazi v. Quazi* [1980] A.C. 744, 807–8 in the following words: "As the Latin words with the label attached to it suggest, the rule applies to cut down the generality of the expression 'other' only where it is preceded by a list of two or more expressions having more specific meanings, and sharing some common characteristics from

which it is possible to recognise them as being species belonging to a single genus and to identify what the essential characteristics of that genus are. The presumption then is that the draftsman's mind was directed only to that genus and that he did not, by his addition of the word 'other' to the list, intend to stray beyond its boundaries, but merely to bring within the ambit of the enacting words those species which complete the genus but have been omitted from the preceding list either inadvertently or in the interests of brevity".

It is possible to add to Lord Diplock's reasons for omitting certain items of the genus from a list. A draftsman may avoid attempting to provide an exhaustive list of the members of a class to which a provision applies —

    (a) because it is impossible to imagine all possible members of the class,

    (b) because the class is so large and diffuse that the attempt would almost certainly fail as the result of an inadvertent omission, or

    (c) because the class is a constantly varying one with members joining and departing.

A helpful example of this rule of construction will be found in *Re Howglen Ltd* [2001] 1 All E.R. 376 Ch. Section 9(2) of the Bankers' Books Evidence Act 1879 refers to ledgers, day books, cash books, account books and "other records used in the ordinary business of the bank". The expression "other records..." might have been sufficiently broad in another context to include notes of interviews between members of staff: but in the context of the other items in the list the court held that the expression could not be construed that widely.

See also *Phonographic Performance Ltd v. South Tyneside MBC* [2001] W.L.R. 400 Ch.

Note however that the only absolute rule of drafting and construction is that there are no absolute rules of drafting and construction. Hence, as Lord Scarman says in *Quazi* at page 284: "If the legislative purpose of a statute is such that a statutory series should be read ejusdem generis, so be it: the rule is helpful. But, if it is not, the rule is more likely to defeat than to fulfil the purpose of the statute. The rule, like many other rules of statutory interpretation, is a useful servant but a bad master".

OWNER.

The word "owner" was defined for the purposes of one section of the Environmental Protection Act 1990 (inserted by a later enactment). Because the definition was limited to that section expressly, the court had to determine what the word "owner" meant where it appeared in a previous section. The court determined that recourse should be had to the legislative history of the provision to be construed, which showed that a series of statutes regulating statutory nuisance had defined "owner" as the person for the time being receiving the rackrent of the premises in connection with which the word was used, whether on his own account or as agent or trustee for another person. So a managing agent could be the "owner". *Camden London Borough Council v. Gunby* [2000] 1 W.L.R. 465 Q.B.D.

P

PAID.
Section 338 of the Income and Corporation Taxes Act 1988 allows a company to deduct yearly interest "paid" by the company in an accounting period from its profits for the period for the purposes of determining liability to corporation tax. Company A lent money to a subsidiary Company B for the purpose of paying arrears of interest on a loan from A to B, so that the payments could be deducted from profits by a purchaser. The Revenue argued that the arrears of interest were not really "paid" since the only purpose of the series of circular transactions was to produce an allowable deduction for corporation tax. The House of Lords held that money was paid by B to A despite being paid out of money lent by A to B for that purpose. The *Ramsay* principle (*W. T. Ramsay Ltd v. I.R.C.* [1981] 1 All E.R. 865) which required courts in fiscal matters to take an overall view of the facts and not to be constrained by the apparent nature of individual parts of a pre-planned series of transactions did not prevent "paid" from being given its ordinary legal meaning here. *Westmoreland Investments v. MacNiven* [2001] 1 All E.R. 865 H.L.

PARENT.
Stat. Def., including a father not married to the mother at the time of birth but who has a residence order in respect of the child, Powers of Criminal Courts (Sentencing) Act 2000 (c. 6), s. 67(2).

Stat. Def., including any person looking after a child, Care Standards Act 2000 (c. 14), s. 4(2).

PARK (IN THE CONTEXT OF A VEHICLE)
Stat. Def., "means leaving a vehicle or permitting to remain at rest" (Terrorism Act 2000 (c. 11), s. 52).

PART.
See SUBSTANTIAL PART.

PARTIAL DEMOLITION.
"There has to be a distinction drawn somewhere, therefore, between 'alteration' and 'demolition of part'. ... So, for example, if the proposal is either to block up a window or to make a new window opening, that would inevitably involve the removal of some existing fabric, but the single operation proposed, taken as a whole, is 'alteration', not 'partial demolition'. Similarly, where an extension is to be built, and a part of the nave wall is to be removed to provide access through to the new building, that is best characterised as 'extension' not 'partial demolition', even though part of the

wall is removed". *In re St. James's Chapel, Callow End* [2001] 1 W.L.R. 835 Worcester Consistory Court, per Mynors Ch.

PARTICULAR REGARD.
See MUST HAVE PARTICULAR REGARD.

PARTNERSHIP.
Stat. Def., excluding partnership which is constituted under the law of a place outside the United Kingdom and is a body corporate, Financial Services and Markets Act 2000 (c. 8), s. 31(5).

PAY.
The concept of pay, within the meaning of the second paragraph of Article 119 of the E.C. Treaty, covered all forms of consideration, in cash or in kind, whether present or future, provided that the worker received it, even indirectly, as a result of his employment relationship with his employer. Family and marriage allowances thus fell within that concept. *E.C. Commission v. Greece* [2000] 1 C.M.L.R. 465 E.C.J.

A Christmas bonus constituted pay within the meaning of Article 141 E.C. regardless of whether it was a contractual entitlement or a voluntary payment, even if paid mainly or exclusively as an incentive for future work or loyalty. *Susanne Lewen v. Lothar Denda* [2000] 2 C.M.L.R. 38 E.C.J.

See also PAID.

PAYMENT.
See PAID.

PERSECUTION.
For the purposes of article 1A(2) of the Convention and Protocol relating to the Statutes of Refugees (1951 — Cmd. 9171 and 1967 — Cmd. 3906), whether ill-treatment amounts to persecution depends not only on the severity of the ill-treatment but also upon there being a failure by the state to afford protection against the ill-treatment. *Horvath v. Secretary of State for the Home Department* [2000] 3 W.L.R. 379 H.L, [2000] 3 All E.R. 577 H.L. (criticised in New Law Journal July 21, 2000 p. 1120).

PHOTOGRAPH.
The term "indecent photograph" in section 1(1)(a) of the Protection of Children Act 1978 (c. 37) is extended by section 7 to include a negative or copy of a photograph, while photograph includes, also by virtue of section 7, data stored on a computer disk which is capable of conversion into a

photograph. The result was that downloading images onto a disk or printing them amounted to making an indecent photograph for the purposes of the offence under section 1(1)(a). *R. v. Bowden* [2000] 2 All E.R. 418 C.A.

See also PSEUDO-PHOTOGRAPH.

PLEASURE CRAFT.
Stat. Def., "any ship of a kind primarily used for sport or recreation" (Finance Act 2000 (c. 17), Sched. 14, para. 21(6).

POINT OF LAW.
Section 204 of the Housing Act 1996 conferred a right of appeal "on any point of law". The Court of Appeal concluded that "a point of law" includes not only matters of legal interpretation but also the full range of issues which would otherwise be the subject of an application to the High Court for judicial review, such as procedural error and questions of vires, irrationality and adequacy of reasons. *Nipa Begum v. Tower Hamlets London Borough Council* [2000] 1 W.L.R. 306 C.A.

POLICE FORCE.
See UNITED KINGDOM POLICE FORCE.

POST OFFICE.
Stat. Def., Postal Services Act 2000 (c. 26), s. 125(1).

POSTAL OPERATOR.
Stat. Def., Postal Services Act 2000 (c. 26), s. 125(1).

POSTAL SERVICES.
Stat. Def., Postal Services Act 2000 (c. 26), s. 125(1); see also Stat. Def., Regulation of Investigatory Powers Act 2000 (c. 23), s. 2(1).

PREMISES.
Stat. Def. (including a vehicle, an offshore installation and a tent or moveable structure), Terrorism Act 2000 (c. 11), s. 121.

Stat. Def., of a particularly wide kind, Child Support Act 1991 (c. 48), s. 15(11) inserted by Child Support, Pensions and Social Security Act 2000 (c. 19), s. 14(4).

PRISON.
Stat. Def., Regulation of Investigatory Powers Act 2000 (c. 23), s. 4(9).

PRIVATE INFORMATION.
Stat. Def., "in relation to a person, includes any information relating to his private or family life" (Regulation of Investigatory Powers Act 2000 (c. 23), s. 26(10)).

PRIVATE TELECOMMUNICATION SYSTEM.
Stat. Def., Regulation of Investigatory Powers Act 2000 (c. 23), s. 2(1).

PRIVATE VEHICLE.
Stat. Def., Regulation of Investigatory Powers Act 2000 (c. 23), s. 48(1).

PRIVILEGED COMMUNICATION.
Stat. Def., Transport Act 2000 (c. 38), Sched. 10, para. 8(2).

PROCURE.
See AID, ABET, COUNSEL OR PROCURE.

PROPERTY.
A milk quota is property within the definition of section 436 of the Insolvency Act 1986 and is capable of forming the subject matter of a trust, although there are limits on how this kind of property can be held or conveyed. *Swift v. Dairywise Farms Ltd* [2000] 1 All E.R. 320 Ch.

A waste management licence under the Environmental Protection Act 1990 (c. 43), being transferable and therefore valuable, was property within s. 436 of the Insolvency Act 1986 (c. 45).

For consideration of the breadth of the term "property" in insolvency proceedings (as used in section 436 of the Insolvency Act 1986 (c. 45)) see *Dear v. Reeves* [2001] 3 W.L.R. 662 C.A. and N.L.J. August 10, 2001, pp. 1219–20.

Stat. Def., Financial Services and Markets Act 2000 (c. 8), s. 112(12) ("includes property, rights and powers of any description").

Stat. Def., "includes property wherever situated and whether real or personal, heritable or moveable, and things in action and other intangible or incorporeal property" (Terrorism Act 2000 (c. 11), s. 121).

Stat. Def., "includes rights and interests of any description" (Care Standards Act 2000 (c. 14), s. 2(3)).

PROPERTY DEVELOPMENT.
Stat. Def., Finance Act 2000 (c. 17), Sched. 14, para. 23(2).

PSEUDO-PHOTOGRAPH.
A pseudo-photograph is defined by section 7(7) of the Protection of Children Act 1978 as "an image ... which appears to be a photograph". Two photographs sellotaped together were a pseudo-photograph: *Atkins v. Director of Public Prosecutions* [2000] All E.R. 425 Q.B.D; [2000] 1 W.L.R. 1427 Q.B.D.

PUBLIC.
It is not always easy to determine when a court or tribunal is sitting in public. But a requirement in the Employment Tribunals (Constitution and Pro-

cedure) Regulations 1993 (No. 2687) for a particular kind of hearing to take place in public was not complied with by proceedings which took place in a room separated from the part of a building normally used for tribunal hearings by a door marked "private" and fitted with a push-button lock. *Storer v. British Gas P.L.C.* [2000] 1 W.L.R. 1237 CA; [2000] 2 All E.R. 440 CA.

PUBLIC-PRIVATE PARTNERSHIP BUSINESS.
Stat. Def., Government Resources and Accounts Act 2000 (c. 20), s. 17.

PUBLIC-PRIVATE PARTNERSHIPS.
Stat. Def., Government Resources and Accounts Act 2000 (c. 20), s. 17.

PUBLIC AUTHORITY.
Stat. Def., Financial Services and Markets Act 2000 (c. 8), Sched. 11, para. 8(2) (including foreign bodies); see also the (variable) list in Schedule 1 to the Freedom of Information Act 2000 (c. 36).

PUBLIC BODY.
Stat. Def., "a government department or a body exercising public functions" (Government Resources and Accounts Act 2000 (c. 20), s. 17(5) & (6)).

PUBLIC FUNCTION.
Stat. Defs., Electronic Communications Act 2000 (c. 7), s. 4(4) ("includes any function conferred by or in accordance with any provision contained in or made under any enactment or Community legislation"); Financial Services and Markets Act 2000 (c. 8), s. 349(5).

PUBLIC HOLIDAY.
Stat. Def., Postal Services Act 2000 (c. 26), s. 125(1).

PUBLIC MEETING.
In the context of section 7 of the Defamation Act (Northern Ireland) 1955 — which grants qualified privilege to newspaper reports of public meetings subject to conditions — a meeting is public if its organisers open it to the public or, by issuing a general invitation to the press, manifest an intention to communicate the proceedings to a wider public. A meeting does not lose its public character because admission is subject to some restriction (as in the case of a press conference). *McCartan Turkington Breen v. Times Newspapers Ltd* [2000] 3 W.L.R. 1670 H.L, [2000] 4 All E.R. 913, H.L.

PUBLIC OFFICE.
Stat. Def., Countryside and Rights of Way Act 2000 (c. 37), s. 85(3).

PUBLIC PLACE.
Stat. Defs., "means a place to which members of the public have or are permitted to have access, whether or not for payment" (Terrorism Act 2000

(c. 11), s. 121); "means any place to which the public or any section of the public has access, on payment or otherwise, as of right or by virtue of express or implied permission" (Criminal Justice and Police Act 2001 (c. 16), s. 16(1).

PUBLIC POSTAL SERVICE.
Stat. Def., Regulation of Investigatory Powers Act 2000 (c. 23), s. 2(1).

PUBLIC TELECOMMUNICATION SYSTEM.
Stat. Def., Regulation of Investigatory Powers Act 2000 (c. 23), s. 2(1).

PUBLICLY-OWNED COMPANY.
Stat. Def., Freedom of Information Act 2000 (c. 36), s. 6.

PUBLISH.
Stat. Def., "means make available to the public at large, or any section of the public, in whatever form and by whatever means" (Political Parties, Elections and Referendums Act 2000 (c. 41), s. 125(4)).

REAL.
A "real prospect" of success (Civil Procedure Rules 24.2(a)) is simply one which is realistic as opposed to fanciful. *Swain v. Hillman* [2001] 1 All E.R. 91 C.A.

RECORD.
Stat. Def., "includes a photographic or electronic record" (Terrorism Act 2000 (c. 11), s. 103(3)).

REFUGEE.
For the purpose of Article 1A(2) of the 1951 Convention relating to the Status of Refugees as modified by the 1967 New York Protocol to be a refugee required a well-founded fear of persecution on Convention grounds and not mere statelessness or inability to return to a country. *Revenko v. Secretary of State for the Home Department* [2000] 3 W.L.R. 1519 C.A.

REGARD.
See MUST HAVE PARTICULAR REGARD.

RESEARCH AND DEVELOPMENT.
Stat. Def., Income and Corporation Taxes Act 1988 (c. 1), s. 837A inserted by Finance Act 2000 (c. 17), s. 68 and Schedule 19.

RESIDE.
Stat. Def., Powers of Criminal Courts (Sentencing) Act 2000 (c. 6), s. 67 ("means habitually reside").

RESIDENCE.
"Habitual residence." A person could be habitually resident in the jurisdiction for the purposes of section 5(2) of the Domicile and Matrimonial Proceedings Act 1973 despite being also habitually resident in another country. The test is whether residence is adopted voluntarily and for a settled purpose throughout a period apart from temporary or occasional absences. *Ikimi v. Ikimi* [2001] 3 W.L.R. 672 C.A.

RESIDENT.
For a discussion of the difficulties of using this word in a legislative context see Dennis Morris, Statute Law Review, vol. 20, no. 2, pp. 111–123, 1999.

RESIDENTIAL CARE HOME.
Stat. Def., Finance Act 2000 (c. 17), Sched. 14, para. 23(3).

RESIDENTIAL PREMISES.
Stat. Def., Regulation of Investigatory Powers Act 2000 (c. 23), s. 48(1).

RESOURCE ACCOUNTS.
This is the new name for appropriation accounts, the accounts which each government department is obliged to present to Parliament each year. Stat. Def., Government Resources and Accounts Act 2000 (c. 20), s. 5(1).

RESOURCES.
Stat. Def., "includes funds, assets, professional skills and any other kind of commercial resource" (Government Resources and Accounts Act 2000 (c. 20), s. 17(4)).

RETAIL SHOP.
Stat. Def., Capital Allowances Act 2001 (c. 2), s. 93(2).

ROAD.
Stat. Def., "means any highway and any other road to which the public has access" (Scrap Metal Dealers Act 1964 (c. 69), s. 4A(7) inserted by Vehicles (Crime) Act 2001 (c. 3), s. 35).

SALE.
Stat. Def., Financial Services and Markets Act 2000 (c. 8), s. 103(7) ("includes any disposal for valuable consideration").

SCHEDULED OFFENCE.
A statutory expression of considerable importance in the context of Northern Ireland: see, now, Stat. Def., Terrorism Act 2000 (c. 11), s. 65 and Sched. 9.

SCOTTISH ADMINISTRATION.
Stat. Def., Scotland Act 1998 (c. 46), s. 126(1).

SCOTTISH LEGISLATION.
Stat. Def., Scotland Act 1998 (c. 46), s. 70(9).

SCOTTISH PARLIAMENT.
Stat. Def., Scotland Act 1998 (c. 46), s. 1.

SCOTTISH SEAL.
Stat. Def., Scotland Act 1998 (c. 46), s. 2(6).

SECURITY.
For a list of activities forming part of the security services industry see the Private Security Industry Act 2001 (c. 12), Sched. 2.

SENTENCE.
A reference to a "sentence" in the United States of America (Extradition) Order 1976 was capable of including a reference to penalties imposed in addition to the custodial element of a sentence. *Re Burke* [2000] 3 All E.R. 481 H.L.

"Sentence of imprisonment", Stat. Defs., excluding certain committals, Powers of Criminal Courts (Sentencing) Act 2000 (c. 6), s. 163; Terrorism Act 2000 (c. 11), s. 80(7).

SERVICE COURT.
Stat. Def., International Criminal Court Act 2001 (c. 17), s. 75.

SERVICE VEHICLE (IN CONTEXT OF ARMY).
Stat. Def., Armed Forces Act 2001 (c. 19), s. 16(8).

SETTLEMENT.
See FULL AND FINAL SETTLEMENT.

SEX.

The word "sex" in the Sex Discrimination Act 1975 includes a reference to sexual orientation as well as to gender, so discrimination on the grounds of sexual orientation falls within the scope of the Act. *MacDonald v. Ministry of Defence* [2001] All E.R. 620 Employment Appeal Tribunal.

SEXUAL OFFENCE.

Stat. Def., Powers of Criminal Courts (Sentencing) Act 2000 (c. 6), s. 161(2).

SHADOW DIRECTOR.

See DIRECTOR.

SHARE.

Stat. Def., including stock and securities, Social Security Contributions (Share Options) Act 2001 (c. 20), s. 5(2)(a).

SHARE CAPITAL.

See ORDINARY SHARE CAPITAL.

SHOP.

See RETAIL SHOP.

SIGNATURE.

See ELECTRONIC SIGNATURE.

SIGNED.

The general position is that at common law a document can be described as having been signed by a person if it is signed in his name and with his authority, but by somebody else. In *Re Horne* [2000] 4 All E.R. 550 CA the court held that there was no necessarily implied displacement of this rule in the use of "sign" in rule 6.1 of the Insolvency Rules 1986 (No. 1925).

SIMPLE CONTRACT DEBT.

Provision is sometimes found in statute that a sum may be recovered as a simple contract debt. This used to be standard and is still found, but it is no longer of much or any significance. Originally it was important where it was desired to give the county courts jurisdiction in the matter: but they now have statutory jurisdiction to deal with recovery of sums due under statute (see County Courts Act 1984). At another stage in the history of this phrase it had significance in respect of limitation periods: but now the limitation periods for contract and statutory debts are the same. The phrase recently acquired renewed — and probably transient — significance, as a result of the decision of the Court of Appeal in *Agodzo v. Bristol City Council* [1999] 1 W.L.R. 1971 C.A. There the court construed the provision for a sum to be recovered as a "simple contract debt" as enabling the debtor to seek a declaration from a county court that the sum was unreasonable despite the fact that there were no proceedings for recovery, since the recovering public

authority had been satisfied by the mortgagee who repossessed the property
in respect of which the sum was owing.

SOCIAL CARE WORKER.
Stat. Def., Care Standards Act 2000 (c. 14), s. 55.
  See also CARE WORKER.

SOCIAL WORKER.
See SOCIAL CARE WORKER.

SPECIALTY.
On the first paragraph of the entry in the main work for SPECIALTY, note
that *Collin v. Duke of Westminster* was applied in *Rahman v. Sterling Credit
Ltd* [2001] 1 W.L.R. 496 C.A.

SPREAD BET.
Stat. Def., Betting and Gaming Duties Act 1981 (c. 63), s. 3(2) substituted by
Finance Act 2001 (c. 9), Sched. 1, para. 1.

STATE (IN INTERNATIONAL CONTEXT).
Stat. Def., Freedom of Information Act 2000 (c. 36), s. 37(5).

STATE (OF PREMISES).
The House of Lords gave (by a 3:2 majority) a purposive interpretation of
the phrase "any premises in such a state as to be prejudicial to health or a
nuisance" in section 79(1)(a) of the Environmental Protection Act 1990
(c. 43) — *Birmingham City Council v. Oakley* [2000] 3 W.L.R. 1936 H.L.
Their Lordships concluded that the Act was directed at the presence in
premises of a feature in itself prejudicial to health as a source of infection,
disease or illness and did not extend to matters of layout or inadequacy of
facilities. Lord Slynn observed (1939 E–F): "Taken literally, it can be said
that the 'state of the premises' is capable of a broad meaning to include a
consideration of the layout, even unavoidable use within the layout. But a
narrower meaning is equally possible. One must therefore look at the
purpose of the legislation and for that consider the history of the legislation
and the context of these words in the Act of 1990 together with previous
judicial interpretations". See also *R. v. Bristol City Council, ex p. Everett*
[1999] 1 W.L.R. 92 Q.B.D., *per* Richards J. — "I have reached the conclusion
that the situation here under consideration is not capable of giving rise to a
statutory nuisance within section 79(1)(a) of the Act of 1990. I accept the
general thrust of Mr Bhose's submissions that this statutory regime is not
intended to apply in cases where the sole concern is that, by reason of the
state of the premises, there is a likelihood of an accident causing personal
injury. In reaching that conclusion, I am influenced more by the legislative
background and apparent legislative purpose of the provisions than by their
actual language". (and note, appeal dismissed [1999] 1 W.L.R. 1170 C.A.);
for a discussion of *Oakley* see N.L.J., May 11, 2001, p. 701.

STEP (IN PROCEEDINGS).

An application for a stay pending an arbitration was not a "step in the proceedings" within the meaning of section 9(3) of the Arbitration Act 1996 if the applicant invoked or accepted the court's jurisdiction, provided that the acceptance was conditional on the failure of the application for a stay. *Capital Trust v. Radio Design T.J. A.B.* [2001] 3 All E.R. 756 Ch.

SUB JUDICE.

For a definition of matters which are sub judice for the purposes of the House of Lords rules prohibiting debate of matters sub judice see the Resolution of the House of Lords recorded in Hansard for Thursday May 11, 2000.

SUBSIDY.

For a definition of what amounts to expenditure (of a company) which is subsidised from public money see Finance Act 2000 (c. 17), Sched. 20, para. 8.

SUBSISTENCE.

Stat. Def., "includes food and drink and temporary living accommodation" (Income and Corporation Taxes Act 1988 (c. 1), s. 200F(5) inserted by Finance Act 2000 (c. 17), s. 58).

SUBSTANCE.

Stat. Def., "any natural or artificial substance, whether in solid or liquid form or in the form of a gas or vapour" (Finance Act 2001 (c. 9), Sched. 22, para. 31(1)).

SUBSTANTIAL.

In context of copyright and copying substantial part of a work — see *Designers Guild Ltd v. Russell Williams (Textiles) Ltd* [2000] 1 W.L.R. 2416 H.L.

Note also that when considering whether a "substantial part" of the typographical arrangement of an edition has been copied the crucial question is whether there has been copying of sufficient of the relevant skill and labour which went into producing that edition — *Newspaper Licensing Agency Ltd v. Marks & Spencer plc* [2001] 3 W.L.R. 290 H.L., [2001] 3 All E.R. 977 H.L.

SUED.

A person "is sued" within the meaning of articles 2 and 6 of the Lugano Convention on jurisdiction (see Civil Jurisdiction and Judgments Act 1982

(c. 27), s. 3A) when proceedings are instituted. *Canada Trust Co. v. Stolzenberg (No. 2)* [2000] 3 W.L.R. 1376 H.L, [2000] 4 All E.R. 483 H.L.

SUITABLE.
"Suitable accommodation". Whether accommodation was "suitable" within the meaning of section 206(1) of the Housing Act 1996 (c. 52) required an assessment of all the qualities of the accommodation in the light of a homeless person's needs and those of his family. Location could certainly be relevant. *R. (Sacupima and others) v. Newham London Borough Council* [2001] 1 W.L.R. 563 C.A.

SUPERVISION ORDER.
Stat. Def., Powers of Criminal Courts (Sentencing) Act 2000 (c. 6), s. 63.

SUPPLIER.
Stat. Def., Transport Act 2000 (c. 38), s. 182(4).

SURVEILLANCE.
Stat. Def., Regulation of Investigatory Powers Act 2000 (c. 23), s. 48(2) to (4).

SURVEILLANCE DEVICE.
Stat. Def., Regulation of Investigatory Powers Act 2000 (c. 23), s. 48(1).

TAKE.

A person took a girl out of her mother's lawful control for the purpose of the offence of abduction under section 2 of the Child Abduction Act 1984 (c. 37) if his actions were an effective cause of the cchild's accompanying him: his actions do not need to have been the sole cause, nor does it matter that consent was one of the other causes. *Regina v. A.* [2000] 1 W.L.R. 1879 C.A.

TAKING.

See Take.

TAX.

Stat. Def., including levy and duty, Finance Act 2001 (c. 9), Sched. 8, para. 9(8).

TAXABLE AMOUNT.

For two recent decisions of the European Court of Justice on the meaning of "taxable amount" in the context of European legislation about VAT and turnover taxes, see *Primback Ltd v. Customs and Excise Commissioners* [2001] 1 W.L.R. 1693 E.C.J. (Case C–34/99) and *Freemans plc v. Customs and Excise Commissioners* [2001] 1 W.L.R. 1713 E.C.J. (Case C–86/99).

TAX AVOIDANCE SCHEME.

See U.K. TAX AVOIDANCE SCHEME.

TECHNICAL.

For what amounted to "technical regulations" in the context of Council Directive 83/189 see *Colim NV v. Bigg's Continent Noord NV* (Case C-33/97) [2000] 2 C.M.L.R. 135 E.C.J. For the same question in a different context see *Snellers Auto's BV v. Algemeen Directeur van de Dienst Wegverkeer* [2000] 3 C.M.L.R. 1275 E.C.J.

TELECOMMUNICATIONS SERVICE.

Stat. Def., Regulation of Investigatory Powers Act 2000 (c. 23), s. 2(1).

TELECOMMUNICATION SYSTEM.

Stat. Def., Regulation of Investigatory Powers Act 2000 (c. 23), s. 2(1).
   See also PRIVATE TELECOMMUNICATION SYSTEM and PUBLIC TELECOMMUNICATION SYSTEM.

TERRORISM.

Stat. Def., Terrorism Act 2000 (c. 11), s. 1.

TERRORIST.
Stat. Def., Terrorism Act 2000 (c. 11), s. 40.

TERRORIST INVESTIGATION.
Stat. Def., Terrorism Act 2000 (c. 11), s. 32.

TERRORIST PROPERTY.
Stat. Def., Terrorism Act 2000 (c. 11), s. 14.

THE LAW OFFICERS.
Stat. Def., "means the Attorney General, the Solicitor General, the Advocate General for Scotland, the Lord Advocate, the Solicitor General for Scotland and the Attorney General for Northern Ireland" (Freedom of Information Act 2000 (c. 36), s. 35(5)).

THEIR.
In a freezing order (what was previously known as a Mareva Injunction) the words "their assets and/or funds" were not apt to cover assets or funds which belonged or were assumed to belong beneficially to someone other than the person restrained. *Federal Bank of the Middle East Ltd v. Hadkinson* [2000] 2 All E.R. 395 C.A.

THREAT OF UNLAWFUL VIOLENCE.
See AFFRAY.

TOOK.
See Take.

TORT.
"Action founded on tort". An action for damages for an infringement of Community rights contrary to section 2 of the European Communities Act 1972 was an action for breach of statutory duty and therefore was an "action founded on tort" for the purposes of section 2 of the Limitation Act 1980. Without express definition, "action founded on tort" should be construed to include any claim in respect of the breach of a non-contractual duty which gave a private law right to recover compensatory damages at common law, whether by reference to Community obligations or domestic obligations. *R. v. Secretary of State for Transport, ex p. Factortame Ltd and others (No. 7)* [2001] 1 W.L.R. 942 Q.B.D.

TRADE DISPUTE.
A dispute between Westminster City Council and a number of employees who were members of a trade union about the proposed privatisation and

contracting out of advisory services was predominantly about terms and conditions of employment and not about public policy. So it was a trade dispute for the purposes of sections 219 and 244 of the Trade Union and Labour Relations (Consolidation) Act 1992. *Unison v. Westminster City Council TLR* April 3, 2001, C.A.

TRADING COMPANY.
Stat. Def., "a company whose business consists wholly or mainly of the carrying on of a trade or trades" (Income and Corporation Taxes Act 1988 (c. 1), s. 13ZA(3)(b) inserted by Finance Act 2001 (c. 9), s. 86).

TRIAL.
A reference to "trial" in an enabling provision in statute was intended to embrace all hearings which form an integral part of the trial process, because it would have made no sense in that context if rules had not been able to make provision in relation to orders in proceedings ancillary to trials. *Ex p.Guardian Newspapers Ltd* [1999] 1 W.L.R. 2130 C.A.

TRUST.
Stat. Def., "includes a trust created by a will" (Political Parties, Elections and Referendums Act 2000 (c. 41), s. 162(6)).

U

U.K. TAX AVOIDANCE SCHEME.
Stat. Def., "a scheme or arrangement the purpose, or one of the main purposes, of which is to achieve a reduction in United Kingdom tax" (Income and Corporation Taxes Act 1988 (c. 1), Sched. 25, para. 4A(3) inserted by Finance Act 2001 (c. 9), s. 82(7).

UNDERTAKING.
In the context of European Community law the concept of an undertaking covers "any entity engaged in an economic activity, regardless of its legal status and the way in which it is financed, and any activity consisting in offering goods and services on a given market is an economic activity". Customs agents were therefore undertakings within the meaning of Article 85 E.C. (they offer, for payment, services consisting in the carrying out of customs formalities and other complementary services). *Consiglio Nazionale degli Spedizionieri Doganali (C.N.S.D.) v. E.C. Commission* [2000] 5 C.M.L.R. 614 E.C.J. (Court of First Instance).

UNITARY COUNTY COUNCIL.
Stat. Def., Local Government Act 2000 (c. 22), s. 55(13).

UNITED KINGDOM.
Stat. Def., including territorial waters adjacent to any part of the United Kingdom, Finance Act 2000 (c. 17), Sched. 6, para. 147.

UNITED KINGDOM POLICE FORCE.
Stat. Def., Armed Forces Act 2001 (c. 19), s. 16(1).

UNNATURAL.
A death by natural causes which should not have been allowed to happen is unnatural within the meaning of section 8(1) of the Coroners Act 1988. *R. v. Inner London North Coroner, ex p. Touche* [2001] 2 All E.R. 752 C.A. [EWCA Civ.383].

USE FOR CONSTRUCTION PURPOSES.
See CONSTRUCTION PURPOSES.

VAN.
Stat. Def., Income and Corporation Taxes Act 1988 (c. 1), Sched. 12AA, para. 3(3) inserted by Finance Act 2001 (c. 9), Sched. 12.

VEHICLE.
Stat. Def. including aircraft, hovercraft, train or vessel, Terrorism Act 2000 (c. 11), s. 121; including any vessel, aircraft or hovercraft, Regulation of Investigatory Powers Act 2000 (c. 23), s. 48(8).

"Goods vehicle", see GOODS VEHICLE.

VETERINARY SURGEON.
Stat. Def., Protection of Animals (Amendment) Act 2000 (c. 38), s. 5(2).

VIOLENCE.
See CRIME OF VIOLENCE.

VIOLENT OFFENCE.
Stat. Def., Powers of Criminal Courts (Sentencing) Act 2000 (c. 6), s. 161(3) ("an offence which leads, or is intended or likely to lead, to a person's death or to physical injury to a person, and includes an offence which is required to be charged as arson (whether or not it would otherwise fall within this definition)").

VOLUNTARY.
"Voluntarily accepted the risk". For the meaning of this expression in section 5(2) of the Animals Act 1971 — and in particular for the proposition that these words are to be read in their ordinary English meaning without too much reference to the long history of the doctrine of *volenti* — see *Cummings v. Granger* [1977] Q.B. 397 *per* Ormrod L.J. at p. 408, applied in *Flack v. Hudson* [2001] 2 W.L.R. 982 C.A.

VULNERABLE ADULT.
Stat. Def., Care Standards Act 2000 (c. 14), s. 80(6).

WAR CRIME.
Stat. Def., article 8.2 of the Statute of the International Criminal Court, done at Rome on July 17, 1998, as applied by section 50(1) of the International Criminal Court Act 2001 (c. 17) and as set out in Schedule 8 to that Act.

WATERCOURSE.
An estuary was not a watercourse within the meaning of section 259(1)(a) of the Public Health Act 1936 (c. 49). *R. v. Falmouth and Truro Port Health Authority, ex p. South West Water Ltd* [2000] 3 All E.R. 306 C.A, [2000] 3 W.L.R. 1464 C.A.

WELFARE SERVICES.
Stat. Def., "includes services which provide support, assistance, advice or counselling to individuals with particular needs", Local Government Act 2000 (c. 22), s. 93(12).

WILFUL MISCONDUCT.
What amounts to wilful misconduct for the purposes of section 20 of the Local Government Finance Act 1982 (audit of local authority accounts) is discussed at length in *Porter v. Magill* [2000] 2 W.L.R. 1420 C.A. In particular, it appears that the persons guilty of misconduct had to know that they were acting unlawfully.

WINNING (IN CONTEXT OF MINERALS).
Stat. Def., Finance Act 2001 (c. 9), s. 48(3).

WOMAN.
See FEMALE.

WOMEN'S SANITARY PRODUCTS.
Stat. Def., Value Added Tax Act 1994 (c. 23), Sched. 7A, Note 4, inserted by Finance Act 2001 (c. 9), Sched. 31(1).

WORK.
In regulation 14a(1)(a) of Council Regulation (EEC) No. 1408/71 a reference for social security purposes to a person normally self-employed in one member state "who performs work" in another state included a reference to any performance of work, whether in employment or self-employment. *Banks v. Theatre Royal de la Monnaie* (Case C-178/97) [2000] 3 W.L.R. 1069 E.C.J.

"In work." A person was "in remunerative work" even during a period of school holidays for which he was not paid, because his employment followed a "recognisable cycle of work" of one school year. *Banks v. Chief Adjudication Officer* [2001] 1 W.L.R. 1411 H.L., [2001] 4 All E.R. 62 H.L.

WORKER.

A pupil barrister was not a "worker" for the purposes of the meaning of the National Minimum Wage Act 1998 (c. 39). *Edmonds v. Lawson* [2000] 2 W.L.R. 1091 C.A.

For the purposes of European Community law and the freedom of movement of workers, a professional player of basketball was a worker. The essence of the test was whether the worker agreed to perform services for a certain period of time for and under the direction of an employer in return for remuneration. The test was satisfied by a player who had signed a contract of employment with a basketball club. *Jyri Lehtonen v. FRBSB* [2000] 3 C.M.L.R. 409 E.C.J.

WORKING DAY.

Stat. Def., Freedom of Information Act 2000 (c. 36), s. 10(6).

WRITTEN-OFF MOTOR VEHICLE.

Stat. Def., Vehicles (Crime) Act 2001 (c. 3), s. 16(1).

WRITING.

"In writing". Stat. Def., including electronic transmissions, Vehicles (Crime) Act 2001 (c. 3), s. 16(2).